EXECUTIVE SEARCH

EXECUTIVE SEARCH

A Guide for Recruiting Outstanding Executives

Richard R. Conarroe
Editor-in-Chief

 VAN NOSTRAND REINHOLD COMPANY

NEW YORK   CINCINNATI   ATLANTA   DALLAS   SAN FRANCISCO
LONDON   TORONTO   MELBOURNE

Van Nostrand Reinhold Company Regional Offices:
New York Cincinnati Atlanta Dallas San Francisco

Van Nostrand Reinhold Company International Offices:
London Toronto Melbourne

Library of Congress Catalog Card Number: 76-20581
ISBN   0-442-21452-9

Manufactured in the United States of America

Published by Van Nostrand Reinhold Company
450 West 33rd Street, New York, N.Y.   10001

Published simultaneously in Canada by Van Nostrand Reinhold Ltd.

15 14 13 12 11 10 9 8 7 6 5 4 3 2 1

Library of Congress Cataloging in Publication Data

Conarroe, Richard R
    Executive search

    Includes index.
    1. Executives–Recruiting. I. Title.
HF5549.5.R44C58   658.4'07'111   76-20581
ISBN 0-442-21452-9

Contributors

From Industry:

Fritz Henry
Senior Consultant
THinc. Career Planning Corporation
New York, New York

Robert W. Lear
Chairman and Chief Executive Officer
The F. & M. Schaefer Corporation
New York, New York

Theodore C. Mullins
Director of Domestic Personnel
Chesebrough-Pond's Inc.
Greenwich, Connecticut

Donald H. Sweet
Director of Employment
Celanese Corporation
New York, New York

George W. Scrimshaw
Former Chief Executive Officer
Columbia Cellulose, Inc.
Vancouver, B.C.
(Now Senior Partner, Washington Executive
Recruiting Group, Inc., Washington, D.C.)

William T. Ylvisaker
Chairman and Chief Executive Officer
Gould Inc.
Rolling Meadows, Illinois

From Executive Search Firms:

Sidney M. Boyden
Director and Founder
Boyden Associates, Inc.
New York, New York

Thomas A. Buffum
President
Thomas A. Buffum Associates
Boston, Massachusetts

Gardner W. Heidrick
Co-Chairman
Heidrick and Struggles, Inc.
Chicago, Illinois

Edmund R. Hergenrather
President
Hergenrather & Company
Los Angeles, California

Preface

While the executive search profession has come to be accepted as commonplace by the current generation of business executives, it is of relatively recent vintage. The first search firm was formed in the mid-1920s, but the movement did not hit its stride of rapid growth until the end of World War II.

Executive search has established itself as an integral factor in corporate enterprise because it fills a real need. The rapid postwar development, beginning in the mid-40s, generated heavy demand for experienced and qualified executives. Corporations found themselves newly in need of general or profit center managers and a host of staff specialists called by strange-sounding names: market research managers, brand managers, quality control managers, long-range planning managers and the like. The era of management decentralization and staff specialization had begun.

As these specialists were not to be found inside organizations that had never carried out such functions before, it was necessary to bring them in from outside the corporate management ranks. The corporations themselves were inexperienced and ill-equipped either to search for or to judge the suitability of candidates.

Recruiting executives from other companies, by whatever techniques, gradually came to be accepted as a good and necessary way to bolster the top management strength of companies. The use of executive search techniques, at first, was the last resort after traditional methods (advertising, employment agencies and word-of-mouth) had been exhausted without success.

similar

Then, starting in the late 1940s, came the rapid growth and influence of the management consultants. In those early days, much executive recruiting was done by these general management consultants as a natural extension of their reorganization recommendations. But soon it became apparent that the skills, technology and backup assistance for executive search activity were of a specialized and different nature from general consulting. Some consultants dropped out of recruiting altogether. Others set up in-house separate departments to perform these services. Soon specialized firms came into existence. First, there were a few individuals, then organizations with offices throughout the United States and eventually abroad in countries where free enterprise flourished.

American industry quickly became aware of the professional services rendered by executive search firms. Foremost among the advantages was the factor of anonymity in the conduct of the search. The opportunity to place their requirements in the hands of highly skilled search specialists relieved the clients of a time-consuming and frustrating employment process. Search firms had at their fingertips information about thousands of executives. They were in a position to interview potential candidates, evaluate their experience and personal qualifications and provide this information to their clients.

As the demand for the services of executive search firms increased, their operations became more sophisticated. The information on executives, worldwide, was programmed into computers, thereby expediting the search process. Research departments were added to provide greater depth and coverage in the search process.

In the 1960s, search firms went international. American companies with overseas operations were faced with the difficult problem of locating executives for top management positions in their foreign operations. It soon became apparent that for search firms to operate overseas successfully, foreign offices had to be established. As a result of this development, executive search extended its scope throughout the free world.

The discipline is now firmly established as the standard mechanism by which industry fills its needs for capable managers. The presidents and chairmen of many of America's largest corporations have been employed through executive search firms. However, management requirements normally involving executive search services include not only positions at the presidential and vice presidential levels, but also departmental and divisional managers, and many other positions that lend themselves to the professional handling available through executive search firms.

Clients of executive search firms are not necessarily confined to industrial companies. The utilization of executive search firms is far broader than industry. Today nonbusiness organizations such as government, foundations, associations, education, insurance, retail, banks and many other nonindustrial companies are regular clients of executive search firms.

In these times we have become accustomed to hearing that change is the name of the game in all society including the business management society. Changing management is one of the strongest, most direct and dramatic ways to change business society. And the organized executive search is by far the most promising technique to employ so as to maximize the chances for success in the executive selection process. So long as this industry can keep pace and develop in keeping with the clients served and the environment within which it operates, there will be a continued growth future for executive recruiting.

Richard R. Conarroe

Contents

EXECUTIVE SEARCH

1
Executive Search: Definition and Scope

Sophisticated corporate managements routinely use executive recruiters today as the best and most economical way to obtain executive talent when they wish to go outside their own ranks.

There are many definitions of what executive search is and does. At its simplest, an executive search is a program, carefully planned and aggressively carried out, to identify and attract the best qualified executive to fill an existing vacancy in the top management of a corporate organization. Two preconditions must exist: first, the corporation must be convinced that its own total interests are best served by going outside, rather than promoting from within; second, it must overcome the belief, now obsolete, that humans are the property of corporations and that there is something unethical about approaching or offering a better opportunity to another corporation's executive.

Focused as it is on finding and attracting for the client corporation specific and carefully delineated talents and experiences, the executive search firm offers as its greatest benefit the near certainty that fully qualified candidates will be presented. If necessary, a search can be kept highly confidential during its process, even though an extremely broad spectrum of possible candidates actually is approached. As specialists in interviewing, appraising, and investigating references, as well as being practicing students of the corporate managerial scene, qualified executive recruiters use a formidable array of skills, all of which help the corporation to make better hiring decisions. Client executives conserve their own time by being involved only at the critical stages of negotiation and decision making. Many consultants are usefully active as go-betweens during less critical negotiations pertaining to compensation and contracts.

Executive search firms, when measured by the traditional terms of monetary volume, numbers of employees and the like, are not sizable or important. As of this writing, only a handful of firms do an annual volume in the millions-of-dollars-per-year range, and only three or four are in the $5-million range. Yet consider the actual influence and power these firms and individuals wield because they directly influence the selection of chief executives, chief operating officers, division presidents and top staff officers in scores of companies whose names are household words in many parts of the world.

Although executive search started as a "better mousetrap" with a low level of technology, today it has become such an important feature of the managerial landscape that it cannot escape attention. As is true of all new technologies, developments, improvements and refinements have been steadily introduced and incorporated.

Notably, the professional association, which is called the Association of Executive Recruiting Consultants or AERC, emphasizes the consulting nature of member–client relationships, calling for the highest standards of professional conduct, responsibility and business ethics.

In the early days, the mere process of identifying talent was considered a great service. Today, the state of the art has advanced so far that this is probably its least valuable service. Computers often serve the larger firms as a means of tracking executive stars and their careers. Specialization is developing around certain corporate needs in such fields as minorities, international, computer and retailing operations. Still other firms have branched out into organization planning, management education, management development and even merger and acquisitions consulting. It appears that the usual trend toward large firms growing larger and small firms becoming absorbed or dying off is underway, although there is no evidence that the level of activity is headed anywhere but up. Some say that of all the services consultants offer, executive search is the one

Many of the most important executive searches take place at the highest levels of management.

corporations do least effectively for themselves, and therefore it has great promise for future security.

Today, small and large corporations all over the free world reach for and use executive search firms, just as though this service had been available forever. Boards of directors are frequently involved when it is necessary to replace either the chief executive or chief operating officer. Investment bankers and investors routinely use executive recruiters, as do bankers themselves. Practically all industries and all but the smallest of enterprises make effective and, in some cases, vital use of this service when appropriate. Even educational and medical institutions are using executive search consultants with increasing regularity, as are federal, state and local governments and their agencies.

This book describes what takes place in the course of an executive search. The reader can obtain a clear differentiation between the various other job-filling techniques and executive search in order to judge which best fits his needs.

THE CASE OF THE DECEPTIVE BALANCE SHEET

By Robert W. Lear

Professional executive search has become much more than just a means of finding people to fill positions in management; it is a tested and proven problem-solving resource for industry.

Here is a case in which a large company ran into an unexpected and critical problem, and was able to call upon the skills of a recruiting firm to solve it. The organization had acquired a $40-million firm in an entirely new industry. The acquired company looked good on paper. It was a mature and effective industry, had a beautiful balance sheet and, except for the last year or two, had been quite profitable.

A new president had just been brought into the parent company. One of his first acts was to visit the prized acquisition. Conditions were shocking: the facilities were rundown and obsolete; the market posture was precarious; controls were virtually nonexistent; the management was tired and old. The company needed professional help, and fast.

The new president talked with a professional recruiter, asking if the recruiter could possibly find for the operating division a president who was an instant miracle worker.

The search consultant asked for all the information about the new company and its immediate and long-term needs. He probed in detail about the job specifications and the personal attributes needed in the job. Above all, he was interested in what the company ultimately wanted to do in the industry. What was the strategic plan?

The corporation's position was that it wanted to acquire several other regional manufacturers in the same business and form a complete new industrial group. Ultimately they would need an executive vice president to head the new group.

Under these circumstances, the recruiter encouraged the president to consider alternative choices: If they could quickly find the right man for the sickly division, fine; if they had trouble, then it might be best to prehire the group head and let him find his division manager, as well as participants in the forthcoming acquisition program. They agreed on the utility of this approach and the recruiter went to work.

In a surprisingly short time, the client had a list of all the key executives in the marketing, manufacturing and general management sectors of the industry. The recruiter knew a little bit about each man, enough to prune the list to about twenty names. Almost all of them were patently better candidates for the group job than for the division post; a decision was made to go after a group vice president.

The recruiter went back to the telephone and began his serious screening. He came up a few days later with the names of three men who might be interested and appeared to be qualified. When asked to arrange for interviews, he tried, but found that all lacked interest, even in talking. Meanwhile, time was running out.

The company examined the qualifications of the three reluctant nonapplicants and decided to concentrate on the one who appeared to be the most susceptible to a strong appeal. After some impassioned selling and a certain amount of monetary inducement, a group executive vice president was hired.

Within a matter of days, he was able to persuade a trusted acquaintance from the industry to take over the sick division. Within a year, he was able to contribute measurably toward the acquisition of three more compatible companies, all of which were well managed and profitable.

The upshot was that within two years the new industry group began to account for nearly 50 percent of the parent corporation's operating profits, and it led the way to a rewarding new period of prosperous expansion and growth in earnings.

2
Filling The Executive Manpower Gap

When Olin Mathieson Corporation (later called simply Olin Corporation) decided to enter the aluminum smelting and marketing business in the mid-1950s, it faced a serious shortage of executive manpower. None of its middle or senior executives had any experience in aluminum. One of the key positions to be filled was that of vice president of sales. Six critical months passed before an industry-trained candidate was located. The man finally hired lasted only six months before he was fired. Thus, more than a year of extremely valuable time was lost in filling what was perhaps the most critical job in Olin Mathieson's expensive new venture.

Whether this staffing failure contributed to the eventual lack of success of the aluminum business and Olin's subsequent divestment of it is a matter of conjecture. Whatever the final impact on end results, Olin failed during a critical period to fill its executive manpower gap. Executive turnover is as certain as death and taxes. In addition, openings result from expansion, diversification, introduction of new technology, reorganization, and a myriad of other reasons. As the economy becomes more complex and diverse, both the need for executives and the rate of executive turnover will increase. Thus, prompt and effective filling of senior positions is an essential and often difficult responsibility of management.

Throughout this chapter the terms *senior positions, executives, top management* and *key openings* are used quite interchangeably to denote that level of the management hierarchy encompassing the two or three top layers of the management structures of most companies. Any attempt at defining *top management* inevitably ends up being imprecise at best and misleading at worst. No claim to precision is made in this instance; the focus of the chapter is on those line and staff positions that are responsible for making policy for the whole corporation, or are accountable for profits at divisional level. Typical titles will be president, vice president, general manager, and other titles indicating responsibility at the executive level.

When a key opening occurs, the aim of every company is to fill the job promptly with an able executive who will stay in place and contribute to the success of the organization. The method actually used to fill the job will vary with the job requirements, the company and its approach to executive recruitment, the industry and the personal idiosyncrasies of the executives responsible for filling the job.

PROMOTION FROM WITHIN

In most companies the first resource considered in almost every instance is *promotion from within.* Allegiance to the principle of promoting its own executives is second only to supporting the free enterprise system in most companies. No company would advocate going outside to fill a key spot if a qualified insider could be found. Such an approach would not only go against the grain of the American success ethic, it would in fact act as a serious demotivator for aspiring employees.

To ensure their capability of filling key positions from their ranks, many companies operate elaborate and expensive management development programs aimed at identifying and nurturing executive talent. Under these programs, young men and women who are identified as possessing potential executive ability are guided through a pre-planned career development program designed to expose the person to the required disciplines, functions, products and responsibilities necessary to prepare him or her for greater responsibilities. It is not unusual for such candidates for top management to be moved through a succession of diverse and unrelated jobs aimed at developing a wide range of management skills and providing the person with the broadest possible exposure to the company's operations.

In one major corporation, recently, a young man with a new M.B.A. started out as a computer software specialist. A short time later he became a financial analyst in the controller's department. Before a year had passed, he was assigned to the treasurer as special assistant analyzing cash management performance. His next assignment, to give him operating management experience, was product manager in the company's plastics division. Two years later he was back in the treasurer's department as assistant treasurer handling cash management and financial planning. At the age of thirty-two, he was appointed treasurer, succeeding his boss who left to become executive vice president of another company.

The above is a fairly typical example of the career path programming that major companies employ. In addition to such on-the-job development, promising young managers are often sent to school, sometimes for up to three months or more, for special training and education. Many universities conduct such programs; perhaps the best known of these is the Harvard Advanced Management Program.

Such industrial leaders as Exxon, Sears, Roebuck, Proctor & Gamble, General Motors, Kodak, DuPont, IBM and Richardson-Merrill have been quite successful over the years with their programs of growing their own executives. Many companies, however, have declined to establish development programs of this magnitude because they either are not convinced that the long-term payoff is worth the expense or they lack the resources and the time to undertake such a program.

CHANGING THE ORGANIZATION TO FIT THE MAN

The commitment to promote from within is often just as strong in companies that do not have developmental programs as it is in those that have them. Indeed, it is not uncommon for companies to realign their organizational structure around the abilities and limitations of existing executives in order to avoid going outside.

Structuring the organization around the man often does more harm to the firm's organizational integrity than it can possibly do good. There are other disadvantages to always promoting from within. Many authorities offer convincing arguments against such a practice. They believe that the infusion of new blood every once in a while prevents inbreeding, narrowness and stereotyped thinking. General Motors' apparent inflexibility and their obvious problems resulting from the wave of consumerism, led by Ralph Nader, has been attributed by some to GM's long practice of promoting its executives from within. It was said that they were all imbued with the same time-worn ideas of what were the right and wrong ways to make automobiles and conduct their business. There was no one available with the objectivity or perspective of an outsider to challenge their thinking.

In addition, there is no evidence to suggest that companies that go outside to fill key positions are less successful than those that always promote from within. The performance of such companies as ITT, Revlon, Xerox, Ford and CBS, all of whom have the reputation of going outside often, attests to the validity of filling senior positions from the outside. Although a few industrial leaders have achieved notable success in developing their own executives, the companies that effectively do so are truly exceptional.

GOING OUTSIDE TO FILL KEY SLOTS

Even those companies with a strong record of promotion from within are occasionally forced to go outside to fill certain key slots. This can occur, for example, when companies enter a new industry or begin serving new markets. When Cessna Aircraft entered the business jet market a few years ago, they had to find a sales vice president who knew the field. None other than Jim Taylor, who had guided Pan Am's successful Falcon program, was lured to Wichita to run the marketing function for the Cessna Citation. Citation was a success right from the start; Taylor is widely credited with playing a giant role in making it happen.

In the final analysis, of course, there is one overriding reason why companies go outside, their preferences and philosophies notwithstanding. It is simply that no executive in the ranks has the requirements to fill the job. Thus in many cases, the only choice is to recruit an executive from outside the company. What then? How does a company go about finding that person with all the qualities required to fill the position? Several methods are used. Some of the more commonly used techniques are discussed below.

Personal Referrals. This may be the first approach employed when a key opening occurs. Usually the chief executive officer or some other top official will inquire among his business acquaintances if they know of anyone who might fit the opening in question. This approach is frequently used where outside directors with wide contacts sit on the board. Their knowledge of possible candidates, especially for high level jobs, is often quite extensive.

The limitations of this method are fairly obvious. First, the extent of possible candidates is automatically limited to the personal knowledge of those queried. Second, the person sought is probably very happily employed now and some sophisticated "selling" will be required to interest him or her in making a change. Third, the company may find it difficult to conduct the rigorous screening and investigation necessary to minimize the risk of failure with a candidate referred by someone close to the organization and its top executives.

Direct Contact With Personal Acquaintances. This is an obvious variation of the above technique and is one that is used fairly frequently when an executive personally knows someone in another company who fits the job in question. Such knowledge may result from business or social contacts, or both, or it may be, as often happens, the result of the two individuals having worked together previously.

Filling a key slot with someone well known to the company no doubt improves the chances of getting the right person. However, it does not guarantee success by any means. This is well illustrated by the much publicized hiring and subsequent firing a few years ago of Semon E. Knudsen as President of Ford Motor Company. Henry Ford II had known Knudsen since early boyhood. Semon Knudsen had been a proven success at General Motors, yet he was a distinct failure in the Ford environment.

Obviously, this resource is useful only in those instances where the hiring executive knows someone who fits the job requirements. If inquiries and personal acquaintances do not produce a suitable candidate, the search for an unknown outsider must be undertaken. This can be approached in several ways.

Advertisements. "Help Wanted" ads are often used to recruit management personnel for middle and lower levels. They are used less frequently to recruit senior executives, although, on occasion, ads for "President," "Vice President," "General Manager," etc. will be seen in the *Wall Street Journal* and the *New York Times* (Sunday edition). Obviously, some companies feel advertising to be a useful vehicle for locating executive talent. The *New York Times* (Sunday financial section), the *Wall Street Journal,* and other Sunday newspapers in big cities are the most frequently used media for executive "Help Wanted" advertisements. Trade magazines are frequently used to advertise middle-management and professional openings, rarely for executive positions. *Fortune* magazine instituted a classified section, including an "Executive Help Wanted" column a few years ago. A check of several issues spanning many months reveals very few advertisements for executive positions.

Many experienced executive recruiters feel that advertising for senior positions is ineffective and unproductive. They cite as drawbacks the following:

1. Most happily employed executives cannot be motivated sufficiently by an advertisement to take the trouble to respond.
2. Few companies are ever willing to run an open ad, i.e., reveal their identity, for an executive position. Often the opening has not been announced inside the company, or the company does not wish to incur the complications of answering every response. (Common courtesy and good business ethics dictate that all responses to an open ad be answered.) Conversely, executives are reluctant to respond to a blind ad.
3. The time required to screen all the candidates, who, on paper, look like "possibilities," can be overly burdensome.
4. Each ad is a one shot effort, and if it doesn't give results, the company has nothing but a cost and loss of valuable time to show for its efforts.
5. No matter how skillfully written, an advertisement is a "shotgun" approach; yet in most cases the requirements for senior positions are so precise and specific that only a "rifle" approach will ferret out the right person.

It would obviously be an overstatement to claim that advertising never works for senior positions. However, this method has far more critics than proponents. Its usage at the senior level appears to be declining rather than increasing.

Situations Wanted Advertisements. Another variation of the advertising approach is to read "Situations Wanted" ads, which are "Help Wanted" ads in reverse. Persons seeking another position advertise (almost always blind) their qualifications and job interests. These ads are most often found in the *Wall Street Journal,* the *New York Times* (Sunday Financial Section), and various trade publications. Obviously, this is not a very productive source for executive talent. Rarely will a person with the requisite skills and background place a "Situations Wanted" ad at the precise time an appropriate opening occurs.

All of the above resources, plus some others, have probably been used at one time or another by every major U.S. corporation. Sometimes these approaches have produced results by turning up the right person at the right time, but, more often than not, such methods are insufficient to identify and recruit top executive personnel.

Third-Party Sources. Since World War II especially, companies with senior level openings have increasingly turned to third party sources for assistance. The two most common forms of third party sources are employment agencies and executive search firms.

Employment agencies are widely used for recruiting professional personnel and others for lower- and middle-level management. They are occasionally used to fill senior level positions. The effectiveness of agencies in producing candidates for top management is often limited, however, due to the nature of their mission. The typical employment agency is able to fill a broad range of jobs quickly and efficiently; hence it usually does not have the time or resources necessary to identify and recruit senior executives. The employment agency is paid *only* after the job is filled. (Their payment is a fee based on the employee's starting salary). Finally, the basic mission of an employment agency is to *find jobs for candidates,* an important and necessary function, and one that employment agencies perform very effectively. This approach is not appropriate, however, for senior level management positions when the mission is to *find candidates for jobs* with very exacting and stringent requirements.

Companies have come to realize that the task of locating, screening and cultivating a candidate for senior management is a complex, time consuming and demanding effort requiring competence, professionalism and confidentiality. Some firms have learned the hard way

A thorough executive recruiting program consumes a tremendous amount of time.

that filling a top job with the wrong person can be the most expensive decision they can make. An effective executive is one of the most productive investments a company can ever make; an ineffective one will be only an expense, the magnitude of which may never be known because of the opportunities that will be missed.

At a recent meeting of stockholders of ITT, someone questioned Harold Geneen's $800,000-plus compensation package. A happy shareholder replied in defense of Geneen: "He would be a bargain at twice the price." And well he would. When Geneen came to ITT from Raytheon in the late 1950s, ITT was an unimaginative, lethargic producer of telephone equipment, doing $765 million in sales and going nowhere. Under Geneen's dynamic and imaginative leadership, ITT became a vibrant, diversified conglomerate that did over $10-billion sales in 1973. Earnings per share have risen from $.95 to $4.17 since Geneen took over. Obviously, ITT recruited the right executive at the right time.

Executive search firms specialize in the task of finding the executive for a specific opening. They are interchangeably called search firms, recruiters, management consultants or, in everyday vernacular, headhunters. These firms are specialists in the complex process of searching out the person who will measure up to all the specifications for a given executive position. The executive search firm, unlike the employment agency, is retained by the client company to conduct a search for suitable candidates. The search firm is paid a fee for its work, whether or not the position is actually filled.

Search firms occupy a unique and justly earned position because an effective search firm avoids the pitfalls of the other approaches and offers advantages that no other recruiting resource can match. Here is why:

1. They are specialists in executive recruiting. They possess the knowledge, the skill and the resources to find the right person, no matter where or how inaccessible he or she might be.
2. They assure confidentiality. As a professional third party representing the client company, search firms can guarantee total anonymity to a prospective candidate as well as to the client company.
3. They are skilled at guiding the candidate and client through the difficult and sensitive phase of actual negotiations. Many promising "engagements" between candidate and prospective employer have been broken because of misunderstandings or lack of communication during the final negotiations of salary, perquisites, etc.
4. The search firm possesses the skill and the objectivity to screen and investigate thoroughly all prospective candidates before the client company ever becomes involved. After all, they will be paid regardless of who is actually hired.
5. They possess the skill to "pre-sell" the reluctant prospect. Often one of the most difficult tasks in recruiting an executive is whetting his interest to that point where he wants to discuss the opportunity with the prospective employer. Search firms are in a uniquely strong position to handle this delicate phase, and they usually possess both the skill and the ethics to avoid overselling or misrepresentation. Indeed, it would be to their disadvantage to misrepresent a situation to a candidate because not only would they risk "turning off" the candidate, but they would also jeopardize their relationship with the client company.

Finally, the executive search firm almost always produces results. It is hired by the client company to fill the position, with the understanding that it will commit its resources to the task until the job is finished. The enormous growth among search firms during the past twenty-five years is dramatic proof that the business is a tailor-made solution to helping companies fill the executive manpower gap.

It will be obvious to the experienced executive recruiter that the above list of executive manpower resources is not all inclusive. Many other techniques have been used by companies to locate and recruit executives. The methods available are limited in fact only by the creativity of the recruiter. Obviously, any method that works should be used, as long as it is both ethical and efficient. Efficiency in this sense must encompass quality (of the candidates produced), timeliness (with which they are produced) and cost per hire. The executive search firm is uniquely suited to deliver consistently regarding all these factors.

THE CASE OF THE RIGHT MAN
WHO WASN'T THERE

Many a business has floundered and failed simply because the right executive was not found and put in charge.

Precision Paper Products, Inc. is a successful, fully integrated pulp and paper company with annual sales in excess of $300 million. It operates one pulp mill in the southeast, which produces Kraft paper and corrugated board. A second mill, located in the midwest, produces bleached sulfite paper board. Thirteen converting plants, which produce corrugated cartons and paper bags, are located near their markets in major cities throughout the east, midwest and southwest.

Growth in sales and earnings has been steady but unspectacular, averaging just under four percent compounded during the past ten years.

General managers head each of the four divisions and operate fairly autonomously. Each division is responsible for its own manufacturing, marketing, accounting, personnel and operating services within fairly broad parameters, but is subject to some basic policies regarding capital spending, budgets, appointment of key people and the like. Although general managers operate with wide latitude, it is well known throughout the company that the chairman and the executive committee consider strong financial control and service to the customer to be the keystones of their success. All operating managers are strongly imbued with these principles.

Dissatisfied with their growth over the last decade, the company began a search for diversification opportunities that would offer more growth and profitability.

The chairman quickly seized on the idea of entering the high quality folding carton business. This is one of the fastest growing segments of the entire paper industry primarily because of the popularity of pre-packaged convenience foods. The market for folding cartons includes just about every segment of the food industry from frozen packaged foods to meat products, cereals and confectioneries. In addition, many household products and toiletries are packaged in folding cartons. Most of the volume is done in bleached sulfite board, which is almost always printed in several colors and has creative design work. This is especially true for cartons used in the food industry.

"It's a natural for us since we already produce bleached board," the chairman told the board members, "and it's a real growth business besides."

Despite some questions regarding Precision's lack of knowledge in folding cartons, the project was approved for three new plants, one each in Atlanta, Pittsburgh and Dayton. The new venture was to be operated as a separate division, like the other businesses.

The chairman felt that the general manager should come from within. In fact, he had someone in mind—Jeff Atkins, vice president of manufacturing of the corrugated division. At forty-one, Atkins had built an outstanding reputation as a bright, no-nonsense doer in the manufacturing organization. A B.S. in mechanical engineering from Carnegie-Mellon and fourteen years of successes in corrugated manufacturing made him a prime candidate for the new venture, at least in the eyes of the chairman. Several board members voiced concern about Atkins' qualifications. They were worried about his lack of experience in folding cartons and suggested that the general manager should come from the folding carton industry.

To appease these members of the board, the chairman agreed to look outside for someone with all the necessary managerial attributes plus experience in folding cartons.

He instructed the vice president for personnel to advertise under a box number in the key trade journals, plus the *New York Times* and the *Wall Street Journal*.

The personnel vice president protested, "I think this will require an executive search firm. There aren't that many people out there with the qualifications we seek. Furthermore, a happily employed person isn't going to respond to a blind ad."

The chairman rejected this idea saying that he preferred to go the advertising route.

More than 200 persons responded to the ads. Six were felt qualified enough for a preliminary interview. None proved to measure up to the specifications when seen face-to-face. The process was repeated with similar results. By now two valuable months had passed. The chairman went back to the recalcitrant board members to report that, as no one could be found who was as qualified as Atkins, he was, therefore, going to appoint Atkins as general manager.

Two years passed while Precision struggled with the folding carton business. Sales in the second year were only sixty percent of plan. Costs were far in excess of industry averages, and worse yet, this division sustained significant losses both years, which erased all of the profit gains from the other divisions.

With growing impatience, the board listened to the grim reports each month. First, there was a quality problem. They couldn't seem to match competition in three- and four-color offset printing, precisely where the big ticket business was. Waste ran six times the industry norm. Problems persisted in the mechanical aspects of the product. Customers complained that the finished product often did not conform to specifications, causing costly jam-ups in their packaging equipment. It seemed that the only way sales could obtain an order was to underbid competition.

At a decidedly stormy board meeting, one of the members said, "Our problem can be defined simply. It's a management problem. I regret the necessity to deal in personalities, but I'm afraid Atkins was not sufficiently prepared to run this business. We entered a business that we knew very little about. The manufacturing process is far more technical and exacting than anything we have ever dealt with. The market is very different. It's a class market where the customer looks more for pizzaz than impeccable service. Atkins' style and attitudes, as well as our own, have been formed and shaped in the corrugated box trade—and incidentally that's our image to most of our customers. Worst of all, he's tried to run the folding carton business as if it were a corrugated business because that's all he knows."

The chairman replied, "You're absolutely right. It's tough to admit, but I made a big mistake when I put Atkins in as general manager. He was severely handicapped by his lack of folding cartons experience. Now I'm afraid I've ruined a good man as well as lost valuable time and money. But, we've got to get moving and turn this thing around. I recently met a very impressive young man with Consolidated Containers—our biggest competitor. He's their sales manager. I'm going to try and hire him as general manager."

"It won't be easy turning this business around," one board member responded, "you'll need the very best manager available and luck thrown in. Our image in the trade is not good. To overcome that will take flawless performance and time. This young man may be a good sales executive but he lacks general management experience. I wonder if he's ready to handle this tough an assignment."

Despite this warning, the young sales executive was hired as general manager.

Two more years passed. Sales improved somewhat, but profits did not. Cost continued out of control, and manufacturing problems persisted.

After almost five years of frustration, and several million dollars in losses, Precision sold its folding carton business to a competitor.

Precision Paper Products faced a serious manpower gap, and for five years failed to fill it.

3
Searching for the Right Executive Search Firm

Executive search firms come in many sizes and varieties, and selecting the right one for a specific assignment requires great care. Not every search firm is suitable for every company or industry. You should give the selection of a search firm the same attention you would give to the selection of the executive who would be filling a position in your company. The search consultant will, after all, be finding and evaluating candidates for you, so his credentials and methodology are vitally important.

There are certain things to look for, certain questions to ask, to make this selection an informed one. Don't take the easy way out by selecting the first search firm whose name comes up in conversation or on the basis of the old school tie; do a little digging.

The first step in the selection process is to look inward and evaluate your own company and the position you seek to fill. A detailed description of the position, as a later chapter will explore in more depth, is a requisite for a good search. It is also a helpful aid in finding a good search consultant, as some search firms do specialize in or emphasize particular industries or management disciplines. A recruiter who really understands the company's function and the requirements of the open position should be selected. A position description should cover both job responsibilities and any character traits considered desirable for the job or for the executive to fit into the company.

Before you select any search firm, consider the extent of the relationship you desire to establish with it. If this is to be a single assignment, with none anticipated for the future, some larger search firms may not be interested in taking it on. Both search firm and client reap benefits from long-term relationships; as the search consultant gets to know a company's activities, style and personnel more intimately, he is that much better able to bring in the most suitable executives. The possibility of a future relationship—or lack of it—should be understood by both sides early in the selection process.

Consider, too, how the responsibilities of search consultant and client company will be delineated during the search. Some companies take a more active role in searches than others. The search consultant you select will want to know the ground rules. Will the consultant handle all reference checks? How many candidates are anticipated? Are any specific evaluative techniques more important than others?

As you prepare to meet with a few search firms, keep in mind that you will be dealing with an individual, not just a firm. From the first exploratory meeting to the completion of the assignment, one individual will represent the search firm in dealings with your company. Try to evaluate the search consultant in the same way that a potential staff member would be evaluated. If you wouldn't want him on your payroll, you may not want him working with and for you in the capacity of recruiter either.

After determining in general what kind of search firm is being sought, you are ready to contact a few likely prospects. Chapter 11 should help in locating reputable recruiters. Try to interview a few different firms, to provide a basis of comparison. And try to allow enough time for the interviews. Giving each search firm prospect at least a half hour to an hour, then spending an additional hour or two with the leading prospect should give you a chance to get to know the recruiter of your choice. This provides an opportunity to develop rapport and to get a feel for how the individual recruiter will represent your company with executive candidates.

The most successful searches, producing the best candidates, tend to be the result of good personal chemistry between client and search consultant. An ability to work together, a mutual sense of

When your company's executive staff already is short-handed, that's no time to place the time-consuming task of finding and recruiting a new executive on the shoulders of one of your own key men.

confidence, leads to a more thorough search. The search consultant should be able to evaluate people by the criteria his client feels are important. The better he knows the client, the better able he is to represent the company well.

There are certain basic lines of questioning to pursue when evaluating a search firm. Each firm will have particular characteristics; determine which firm's set of characteristics fits best with your company and with the individual search that is planned.

Knowing what to look for in a search firm will help in the decision-making process. The main factors to consider are presented and discussed below.

EXPERTISE

Like any professional, the search consultant should be judged primarily on his knowledge of his profession and his proficiency in practice. A search consultant's expertise, however, should extend beyond his own business to his client's. Most consultants do have a broad knowledge of business, industry and the executive job market, yet they sometimes specialize in certain industries and management disciplines as well.

Check on the background and experience of the search consultant. During discussion of the assignment, give him opportunities to display his understanding of your particular field or of the discipline involved. He will do a better job of "selling" your position to the best candidates if he has a thorough knowledge of your industry and of what the executive who fills the job will be called upon to do.

A consultant who is highly specialized in one field may present one problem, however. He may have many clients in that field—so many that the larger part of the industry is off limits to him as a recruiter. To assure that a sufficient number of qualified candidates will be available, assemble a list of the important companies in your industry. Go over the list name by name with the search consultant to determine how many he would be able to use as sources.

SIZE

Since a single individual basically handles a search assignment, a one-man shop may be as effective as a larger one. Any size firm has both pluses and minuses for the individual client, and evaluations have to be made in terms of the specific assignment.

A larger firm will generally have greater staff support and research capability than a small one. If the position to be filled will have a large pool of potential candidates, the more sizeable multi-office firm may be able to identify them more quickly.

A small firm, on the other hand, may be able to preserve better and more fully the confidentiality of an especially delicate assignment. Because it has fewer clients, the smaller firm may also have more sources of candidates. In highly concentrated industries, where candidate selection may be limited, this factor can be very important.

An increasing concern with regard to size is which member of the search firm will be handling the actual assignment. Whether the firm has two or twenty consultants, be sure that the one you talk to is the one who will handle the search. Sometimes the senior expert will meet the client, but an associate with less experience and expertise will be sent out to meet the candidates.

Check, too, to ensure that the search firm is not in the middle of overlapping assignments that would send the same candidates to your company and others simultaneously. This, too, is more likely to happen with a large, geographically dispersed search firm.

LOCATION

Geographical proximity is not the most important factor in selecting a search firm, but it is worth taking into account. Regular and accurate communications between client and search firm are important to the outcome of the search. You want to be sure the firm you choose will be accessible for consultation, particularly in the later, decision-making period of candidate selection.

METHODS

Try to get some idea of the methods used by each individual search firm you interview. You don't need a minute-by-minute account of a firm's procedures, but you are entitled to answers to certain basic questions. Some of the following may be pertinent to the search assignment:

1. How much use is made of source letters versus direct contact?
2. Does the firm have wide contacts in your industry?
3. Will candidates be contacted mainly at work, or out of the office where they may feel freer to talk?
4. What percentage of time will be spent looking for names and what percentage actually contacting prospects?

5. How extensive are the search firm's files and its research capability?
6. How much time does the consultant spend with the candidate before presenting him to you?
7. How much information will the consultant provide to you before you meet the candidate? (You should receive a good biographical sketch of the candidate plus the consultant's evaluation of him.)
8. What steps does the consultant take to insure the confidentiality of your search assignment?

REPUTATION

Evaluating a consultant's reputation will require some effort and enterprise, but doing some reference checking is critical. After meeting at length with a search consultant, you will have formed your own judgments. It is always prudent, however, to supplement your own subjective view with comments from others.

Because of the confidential nature of the business, most search firms consider the names of their clients privileged information. However, names of a few satisfied clients will usually be provided as references. To get a broader and possibly more candid viewpoint, it is appropriate to ask the search consultant whether he is known by certain executives of your acquaintance who use search consultants. Try to contact at least one reference you are familiar with personally.

When checking out a search firm, be sure to determine the names of the individuals who have handled search assignments for the reference. The reputation of the firm in general is much less important to you than the reputation of the individual who will be handling your project. It is his skill, integrity, personality and discretion that will play a large role in determining the outcome of your search assignment. Try to find out the length of the relationship between the search consultant and the reference-client being contacted, and whether the reference has used other search firms. Ask how he would compare them.

If references are satisfactory, get back to the search consultant and try to pin down the assignment. Determine the degree of his interest in your company and in the specific search in question. Find out, if possible, whether he has the time available to take on this assignment and how much of his time and efforts you will receive.

It is, of course, impossible to know whether you have selected the right search firm until the results are in. The results are proven by the executive hired and his ultimate performance on the job. But if you have done a careful and thorough job of selecting a search firm, have chosen a man with whom you feel comfortable and confident, your selection was probably a good one.

THE CASE OF THE POORLY SEARCHED SEARCH FIRM

An executive search firm can save a company a lot of time and money in filling its manpower needs, but selecting the right firm is something companies have to work out carefully for themselves.

A medium-sized manufacturing company, which had relied on newspaper advertising to find new staff, determined in one particular instance that such a course was inappropriate. Instead, the company decided for the first time to retain an executive search firm.

The company's leaders asked business acquaintances for suggestions. Few of these sources were really knowledgeable, but all provided names. Trying to do a thorough job, the prospective client talked to no fewer than six consulting organizations of varying size. The firm selected was picked on the basis of its dynamic presentation. Only later would the company learn it should have studied the quality of the staff and support function, plus the firm's performance record. No reference checking was done.

The manufacturing company found in the course of the ensuing search that the consultant selected had no realistic concept of the client company's business, nor did it really understand the type of individual who would fit the particular environment. The result, after seven months of fruitless effort, was a terminated assignment and an unfilled vacancy. The manufacturing company had failed to realize that a better search for a search firm itself would undoubtedly have enhanced the prospects for success.

In another case, a similarly dissatisfied company decided to choose the biggest search firm it could find, believing it would also be the best. No screening was done, however, and the one major firm interviewed pointed to its extensive files and said it might already have the answer to the client's problems.

Months passed without acceptable candidates being presented. Discussions between client and consultant provided a rude awakening for the client. Assignments that involved qualifications matching individuals already in the consultant's file would be done well, but those involving true search work were beyond his capability.

At that point, the client realized that search—not files—was the name of the game. The assignment ended with a termination, and the client then turned to consideration of several firms, some large and some small, but all of whom, as reference checking demonstrated, were indeed competent at search work.

One small manufacturing company seeking an executive search firm purposely chose a small firm because it thought the virtue of its size would allow it to devote extra personalized attention to the search itself.

The company had heard that with large search firms there was danger of overlapping assignments. The company also feared it would just be another account in a large search firm's portfolio. It suspected the same candidates would be sent to several companies simultaneously by a large search firm creating difficult conflicts.

The small firm that was hired, however, failed in its task. The candidates for the particular job were spread geographically across the country. Problems developed and it became clear that the small firm didn't have the capability to do the job.

Subsequently, the company in need of an executive went to a larger firm and eventually got the person it was looking for. The company also learned that most reputable search firms have an internal intelligence system. Through it, all associates are informed of any assignment or any individual with whom a member of the firm is involved as a check against overlapping work.

The size of the search firm or any one single factor alone should not be the deciding element in selecting a search consultant.

4

How an Executive Search Firm Works

Executive search is an exacting and highly specialized management technique. It is applied with varying degrees of similarity and difference by individual firms, but almost all search firms follow certain fundamental procedures to reach the desired goal. Only in extremely rare instances can an executive recruiter fill an assignment simply by going back to his office and picking likely candidates out of a file.

As no two jobs, individuals or companies are the same, so no two executive searches are the same. If all searches were alike, a recruiting effort could be programmed and the search done by computer. But this is not the case. There is, however, a basic approach, a starting point for each individual executive search.

THE STARTING POINT

The starting point is gaining information from the client company. The recruiter must learn as much as possible about the client company and the position to be filled. Why is the position open? Did the last man fail? If so, why? Can the job be filled from the inside? If not, why not? The dynamics, the tensions, the general atmosphere of the organization and the personalities of its executives are all a part of the inputs needed for a good search. Any corporate problems—personnel, financial, or whatever—should be presented to the recruiter.

The recruiter also needs a very specific job description and candidate profile. Many times the client has not yet clearly defined the job he seeks to fill, and the recruiter can apply his experience to help the client fill in the gaps. By zeroing in on the job in terms of responsibilities, working relationships, company structure, work experience and educational requirements, the search firm can more quickly and precisely identify the people who are best suited for the job.

Any limitations of the job itself also belong in the initial description. If the job is a dead end, the search firm must know it, and select prospects accordingly. There is no point in placing an ambitious young man in a dead-end position.

The position and man (or woman) descriptions must cover all bases. Personal qualities that are desirable for the job—dynamic self-starter, well-spoken, congenial, well-groomed—should be spelled out in the candidate profile. Often the most important qualities for a candidate are the unwritten ones. Every company has a certain chemistry, and the search firm must find this chemistry in suitable candidates, so as not to waste everyone's time. A candidate with the right work experience but the wrong chemistry is unlikely to be hired, and, if hired, is unlikely to succeed.

Compensation, including salary, stock options, insurance, pension plan and any other financial benefits, should also be specifically outlined at the outset of the search.

It cannot be too strongly emphasized that without the fullest cooperation from the client—without the broadest input of information—the chances for success in the search are limited. Finding the best man for a job requires intense knowledge of the position and the company.

DEVELOPING PROSPECTS

With as much information in hand as he can possibly obtain from the client, the recruiter prepares to begin the search itself. The search firm works up a general plan that involves making preliminary contacts, conducting preliminary interviews and preparing preliminary reviews for the client, which are continually updated to

Before the executive search begins, the recruiter will probe deeply into the company to find out what kind of executive the company really needs; this may be considerably different from what people in the company think and say they need.

keep the client informed of progress made—all this before actual client–candidate interviews are arranged.

Over the years, most established search firms have accumulated exhaustive files containing thousands of résumés of executives in every field. Some firms have their files computerized. These files are vital to a search firm and are one of the important tools of the trade. The listings fall into three separate categories: contacts, prospects and references.

The list of prospects will probably include the backgrounds of several executives who may be suitable for and interested in the position in question. A search of the file will usually turn up prospective candidates with the proper qualifications, whom the recruiter will then contact by letter or phone to determine the interest they may have in the position. If no interest is expressed, the recruiter will ask the prospect for suggestions of other candidates in the field or industry.

Probably the largest and most extensive of the categories is the file of contacts—people with whom the search firm has established a reciprocal relationship of confidentiality, and who can be contacted for recommendations of prospects for a particular search. A search firm's contact may be someone who is active in a pertinent trade association, who has worked for a target company (a company recognized as a likely source of candidates) in the past or who works in a closely related industry.

Contacts may also be in the same industry, but unsuited for the job in question because of age, temperament, particular field of expertise or even lack of interest. Still, they are most helpful in recommending likely prospects. Good contacts are vital to the recruiter; he cultivates them, appreciates them, thanks them, but does not pay them. They are an important means for gathering information about companies and individuals in a discreet manner, which has tacit approval in the executive search field.

Because of a long, carefully developed relationship, the search firm knows which of its contacts are most reliable. A good contact will provide the best names in a field, rather than those he knows are looking for a job. Some of this information may also be available in a recruiter's files, but, since files become dated quickly, personal contacts give better information.

The search firm's files are only a starting point for potential candidates. Any full-scale search requires a study of companies within the industries in which candidates are likely to be found. If a client has said, "Here are the main companies in our field, the companies most likely to have the person we are looking for," the search firm can center its search in this area and save some time and effort. In some fields, only a narrow range of candidates will be suitable for a job. If, for instance, a company is looking for a man to head research and development in biochemicals, it is obvious that only someone currently in biochemistry would be considered. If the job is in a consumer products marketing field, the area of selection is likely to be greater, as a larger variety of companies may have executives with the right experience.

A carefully selected mailing list might be used to obtain names of top people in a particular industry. If, say, a search is on for a particular kind of sales person, letters might be sent to purchasing agents in that industry; the letters are designed to elicit the names of top sales people. The name of the client company is, of course, not revealed, but a general description of the job available may be included.

Public data—directories, lists, meeting programs—can be used as sources for this type of information as well. The development of such lists is a time-consuming process that must be handled with discretion and integrity.

Pinpointing the companies is not as difficult as identifying those individuals within the companies who are at the right level and who may be interested in moving on to a better position.

In mid-1974, for example, all the better companies in the engineering and pipeline industries were very busy. All were aggressively seeking additional personnel at all levels, even, in some cases, the presidential level. Growth opportunities for good employees were there in all these firms and their rates of compensation were all similar. However, many of the prospective executive candidates for these companies were located in out-of-the-way locations and were hard to track down. An enormous amount of research and contact work was needed for a recruiter to find a man for whom a job change made sense. The extent of the research needed in such cases is one reason companies turn to executive search firms.

MAKING CONTACT

Once the recruiter has names, he must get in touch with potential prospects. Some executives, particularly those who are always on the road, are hard to contact or to interview; thus travel is often a big part of the recruiter's job. A recruiter must be persistent, pleasant, perceptive and able to make judgments quickly about pursuing an individual prospect.

When a search consultant talks with a potential prospect, he must try to ascertain what factors—money or other compensatory benefits, flexibility, mobility, increased responsibility, improved surroundings—are likely to induce the man to consider a change. In some instances, the motivation to change is not there, but if the position offers greater opportunity, most executives will at least listen.

On rare occasions an executive prospect will show reluctance even to engage in a discussion about a possible job change. A skilled recruiter will find a way to get such people to listen at least to a description of the opportunities. At the same time, the recruiter will determine whether the prospect is worth pursuing further.

Preliminary interviews are conducted for the purpose of assessing prospective candidates. A general discussion of the past experience and an evaluation of the prospect's relative position in the organizational structure help the recruiter get to know the person involved, and his perceptions of himself and his business. Through such conversations, the recruiter may also get additional perspective on the job to be filled. A client may have asked a search firm to find a vice president of finance, but if someone turns up with a combined financial and legal background, this may be a plus. Although the prospect may turn out to be wrong for the particular search being undertaken at the moment, he may still go into the prospect files for follow up when something slightly different comes along.

PRELIMINARY REVIEWS

Following preliminary interviews with a number of likely prospects, the recruiter will eliminate certain names, reevaluate others, and come up with a few promising candidates. He will then conduct preliminary reviews of the search's status with the client, discussing the backgrounds of his recommended candidates with the client for the client's reactions. This shoe-fitting process is very important. The client's response to these prospects enables the recruiter to detect certain biases the client may not have revealed in earlier, more general discussions. By watching how the client reacts to specific people with specific backgrounds, the recruiter can get a clearer idea of the man to go after and the kind of man to shy away from.

These preliminary reviews have the added importance of a continuing client–search firm contact that underlies any good search. A good search firm will keep the client up to date on its activities, successes or problems, and the client should also let the recruiter know of any changes that have evolved in its own needs. A search goes more smoothly when all involved are informed of the current realities of the dynamics of the executive job market, and of compromises that may have to be made.

During these preliminary reviews, the recruiter may make some suggestions about changes in the type of candidate being sought. This is most likely to happen when the client has not given very specific job descriptions or candidate profiles, or when the client has not been very specific in his early interviews with the search firm.

The question of salary may arise during these reviews. The recruiter may have discovered during his preliminary interviews with prospects that the salary range discussed with the client is not high enough to attract the caliber of candidate being sought. Particularly in cases where the client is not experienced in top-level hiring, this may not become apparent until the market has been researched.

In some cases, although infrequently, the search consultant will discover, and so inform the client, that the best man for the job may be in the firm already. After assessing the market carefully, that may be the inescapable conclusion. Since the contacts who are tapped do not know who the client company is, several may suggest a man within the client's organization. If the client agrees and promotes that man, the search is terminated.

INTERVIEWING TECHNIQUES

After eliminating certain prospects as a result of the preliminary interviews and the reviews with the client, a more intensive stage of interviewing begins. Interviewing techniques vary among search firms, of course, but the skilled recruiter knows that there are certain basic questions that need to be answered about a candidate. Is he qualified technically? Does he have the administrative know-how? How is he motivated? How does he function under pressure? How will his personality mesh with those of his future colleagues?

In attempting to decide upon the best candidate from every perspective, the recruiter must be a careful and objective listener and observer. If the position to be filled is in general management, the interviewer looks for decisiveness, ability to communicate, ability to solve problems, ability to delegate authority when necessary and accept authority when necessary—and to know the difference. He will also look for real evidence of success on the job.

In the case of a marketing manager, research director or production manager, the same basic criteria will be followed with obvious technical variations dependent upon the needs of the position to be filled. The recruiter will also look for specific kinds of experience in previous positions that the candidate must have in order to fill the client's needs.

An interview will not answer every question, but, combined with reference checks, it will help the recruiter to form a total picture of the candidate. Often a recruiter will want to meet with the candidate more than once to be sure that extraneous factors did not affect his initial impression. The client wants to know negative as well as positive characteristics of each candidate; every person has both, and it is best that they be spelled out in the beginning.

CHECKING REFERENCES

After intensive interviews with the candidates, but before introducing them to the client, the recruiter will begin to speak with others about the prospect—check his references. Initially he will be limited to references provided by the prospect himself, and these references are likely to be totally favorable. However, from these references, the recruiter will obtain others, known in the business as second-generation references, who will more likely provide a more objective picture of the candidate. These so-called second-generation references may also be people with whom the candidate has done business away from the job, people with whom he has had social contact, someone he studied under, someone he roomed with or associates in business organizations.

This is a delicate area and should be approached with utmost confidence and caution; it is vital that the prospect not be embarrassed or have his current job jeopardized as a result of these checks. In addition, the client company often wants its search to remain confidential at this stage.

For these reasons, some recruiters do not make thorough reference checks until the client has interviewed a candidate and expressed an interest in going further. Most candidates will not present themselves falsely on a factual basis, but their perceptions of their own strengths and weaknesses are likely to be different from others' views of them.

The emphasis put on reference checks varies among different search firms. Some consider such checks of vital importance, an opportunity to project a man's performance in the job in question based on the marks he has made in the past. Others view reference checks as analogous to title searches, a safety measure to be sure that all is as it seems to be. These variations are actually rather

When a candidate submits his résumé and other personal data to a company through an executive search firm, he has a right to expect that the information will be held in complete confidence. Too wide dissemination could undermine his present position.

subtle, as all search consultants will handle reference checks discreetly and carefully, and evaluate them thoroughly.

In one case, a candidate appeared ideal until careful checking revealed that he had always relied heavily on the man below him.

In the one position where he had no number-two man to save him, he lost the company $300,000. Because the position for which he was being considered called for a decisive self-starter, able to work independently, careful checking ruled this candidate out of consideration.

The skill and tact of an experienced recruiter are needed for these checks in order to probe accurately the candidate's strengths and weaknesses. Honest responses are sought; the recruiter tries to speak with people who really know the individual. A good recruiter will try to speak with a number of people, whether it be early or late in the selection process. The larger the number of views obtained, the truer the emerging picture is likely to be. The client may even want to do some reference checking on his own, through his own contacts, once a candidate is being seriously considered.

A company is well advised to pay close attention to the detailed background report a search firm prepares for serious candidates. In one recent instance, a search firm learned the hard way the consequences of the failure of the hiring company to adjust properly to what had been revealed in reference checking about the man who was hired. The top marketing executive the company hired came highly recommended for intelligence, creativity and innovation, but references pointed out over and over that he worked best under strict control from above. His new employer failed to provide such control, and in six months the marketing department was in chaos and the company was forced to fire the executive.

Prior to a client's face-to-face interviews with the candidates, the recruiter should discuss each serious candidate with the client in depth. This involves going over the background, interviews, references and the pros and cons of each individual. The recruiter will also suggest some dos and don'ts for getting the most out of the forthcoming client–candidate interviews.

CLIENT INTERVIEWS

Most client companies, because of their confidence in the search consultant, will interview those candidates he recommends. In general, the search firm will have reduced the number of candidates to relatively few for the client to interview, probably no more than five.

When a client interviews a candidate, he must remember that the candidate is not necessarily seeking a job. The company is, rather, seeking an executive. The company is selling itself and the candidate may or may not be selling himself. Any candidate who gets this far is almost certain to have the required technical qualifications. It's the personal chemistry that is to be tested in the interview. If, for instance, the candidate is an intuitive, fast-thinking person, and the client a logical, step-by-step person, there is very little chance for good communication. That's what the interview is designed to find out, and setting aside enough time for a serious conversation will be most productive for both sides. Afterward, both should give their impressions to the search consultant. If the client and candidate didn't jell, the recruiter must be able to determine why so that the same problem does not come up again. If the interview has gone well, subsequent talks are in order.

Once the client has narrowed the field to the top two or three candidates, the recruiter will usually interview each again. This is to find out what reservations, if any, client and candidate have about each other, and to try to work out any problems. Final reference checks may also focus on any problem areas. If all angles look good, the search consultant will encourage candidate and client to talk further and to try to work out a specific arrangement.

The final decision and actual hiring are the responsibility of the client. But the search consultant is often asked by client, candidate or both, to assist in working out the details. Misunderstandings can cause the arrangement to fall through at this point, and, as an interested but objective third party, the recruiter can help both sides get questions answered and reach an equitable agreement.

FOLLOW-UP

A search consultant does not close the books on a placement when hiring is completed. As a conscientious professional, he keeps in touch with his client and, with the client's permission, with the man he placed, on a regular basis. Checking with the client after three months, six months and a year, as to how things are going allows the recruiter to learn whether there are any problems he can help to iron out.

A placement that satisfies both client and candidate is extremely

Although the job candidate may present himself at your office for an interview, don't make the mistake of treating him like a job seeker. He probably has a good job now and is interested in talking with you only because your search consultant has told him of your interest in him.

important for the search firm. If the placement works, the search firm is likely to be engaged again by the client, and it is that long-term aspect with which a search firm is concerned. When the *best* man, not just *a* man, is found for the position in question, everyone's best interests are served—those of the client, the candidate and the recruiter.

THE CASE OF THE ILL-DEFINED JOB

The contribution of the executive search professional is not restricted to finding superior people. Some of the consultant's most important work may be done before the search begins, as he helps his client to define precisely what the company needs.

Many organizations have general ideas about their needs, but when it becomes necessary to put these needs on paper, conflicts and ambiguities arise. This sort of incomplete grasp of the distinct requirements of an executive position can lead to delays in filling the job and disappointments after it is filled. A competent search firm will make sure at the outset that the client's needs are clearly defined.

When this important step is not handled expertly, problems mount. Take the case of a medium sized pharmaceutical company that was looking for a new marketing executive.

The company's product line was losing out to competition. Costs were going up. A new product line was being considered and a new man was needed to head the operation.

Management decided it wanted someone with strong sales experience in the pharmaceutical field, who would be ready to take over a new division. The executive recruiter—who later admitted that he should have pressed for more detailed discussion at the outset—accepted management's seemingly cogent criteria.

A search was launched. The company was introduced to several candidates with good backgrounds in pharmaceutical sales who appeared seasoned enough to be ready to take over a division.

The candidates were interesting; they matched all the established criteria. However, management was only partially satisfied with them. Curiously, the one candidate who did score high with management had small experience in the pharmaceutical field but great experience in management. The executive recruiter sensed the problem.

After involved discussion between the recruiter and members of management, it became clear that the company actually had all the pharmaceutical experience it needed within its own ranks. What the company really required was someone who could implement decisions and manage effectively. Attention shifted to the candidate with the strong management background. He was hired—and he was able to transform the new division into a strong success within eighteen months.

5
Working Successfully with a Search Firm

As many executives and all executive search consultants know, technical competence is not the final determinant of a candidate's success or failure in a new position. Personal chemistry looms as far more significant.

The same holds true for the client–search firm relationship. Hiring a well regarded, highly qualified recruiter will not necessarily assure success unless you, the corporate client, use the recruiter to best advantage. Together, you must move the relationship from one of cooperation to one of mutual respect and complete confidence. This goal can be accomplished only if sufficient time is expended by client and consultant to know each other's philosophies and preferences, and to view each other as business friends.

This rapport will prove invaluable as the search progresses, not only for maintaining open lines of communication, but as the means of quickly and easily overriding differences of opinion that might otherwise serve as barriers to your common objective of placing a qualified candidate on your management team.

What is the alternative to a healthy client–consultant relationship? At the least, unnecessary outlays of time and money on the part of both parties; at the most, failure of the search.

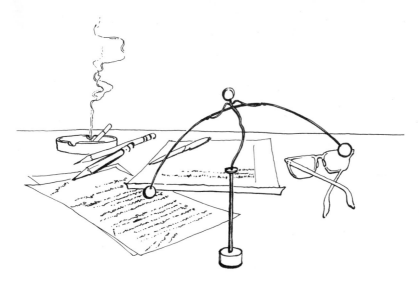

There are few easy decisions in executive search. The right decision comes after extensive fact-finding, analysis and insight. Even then, a certain amount of luck helps.

ESTABLISHING THE RELATIONSHIP

Once you as the client have convinced yourself that a certain recruiting organization can handle the specific search you have in mind, a meeting at your headquarters with the senior recruiter and his staff person, if he chooses to bring one, is mandatory. This meeting may take up an entire day. Be prepared to invest your time in it.

Prior to this initial meeting, both client and recruiter need to do their homework. The client will find it advantageous to confer with other key internal personnel to establish a concensus as to what kind of executive is required from outside, and why. The age and the education of the individual sought, what his title and responsibilities will be and what industrial and functional experience he should bring to his new post are primary considerations to review.

The consultant, in turn, will marshal as much information as he can relative to the company itself, its top executives and the industries in which it participates, in order to prepare questions he believes to be germane to his efforts.

At this initial meeting, consultant and client must communicate completely and candidly. Occasionally clients—especially those who are working with a recruiter for the first time—hesitate to reveal the innermost workings of their company. Yet confidentiality is the name of the game; reputable recruiters respect the confidential nature of their work, or they enjoy no repeat business and eventually no business at all. Without knowing all the facts, the recruiter simply cannot do a successful job. If a client feels he can't trust the recruiter's discretion, he's better off either changing search firms or canceling the search.

WHY THE OPENING EXISTS

To do his best work, the recruiter needs to know why the opening exists: is it because of retirement, creation of a new post or the voluntary (or involuntary) departure of the incumbent? The recruiter will want to know what, if anything, has already been done to identify suitable candidates.

Further, the recruiter will want to know about the executive team, particularly as it applies to the position he will be working to fill. To whom will the successful candidate report? The recruiter should meet this person face to face. Were any other executives, internal or external, considered for the job? Why were they deemed unsuitable? If they rejected the opportunity, what were their reasons? The recruiter may also ask to meet the incumbent in the post, if feasible.

Another person with whom the consultant should be certain to spend some time is the person in your organization who will make the actual decisions during the search. Few things in the search process are more frustrating than spending the day with a CEO, only to hear him say, while shaking hands goodby, "You've got a good handle on our situation. Just be sure to keep Charlie in the Consumer Products Division informed, as he'll have a big say in our decision." Charlie?

During this first meeting, the recruiter will have his antennas out, tuning in on nuances that will help him further understand the client organization's history, business philosophy, style and goals. Despite his earlier preparation, he'll need this first-hand knowledge in order to serve as the client's well-informed spokesman before the outside world of sources and prospects.

Additionally, when the consultant departs this initial session, he should be armed with annual reports, product literature, investment analysts' reviews of the industry and/or company, organization charts, personnel booklets concerned with employee benefits and any other materials helpful in attracting prospects to the opportunity.

As his contribution to open communication, the recruiter can be expected to go over the ins and outs of the search process in detail. (This is not a bad idea even for the third, fourth or fourteenth search his client has experienced.) One item that needs to be settled in advance is the client's time requirement. Most hiring organizations want the new executive "as soon as possible," and should come to an understanding with the recruiter at the outset of the search activity as to when candidates will be presented.

It is almost impossible to judge accurately the caliber of an executive by his résumé alone.

TYPE OF PERSON REQUIRED

One of the more ticklish areas of the client–consultant relationship is the establishment of specifications for the job at hand. The easy part is deciding upon fundamentals such as experience, age range, education and compensation. Beyond these considerations, however, both the client and consultant will save time, money and frustration by seeing that the recruiter understands the type of person who will succeed in the client's environment.

Most clients have "hidden" specifications. Perhaps, for example, the client once worked with a group of Ivy League graduates, and, as an alumnus of a midwestern state university, he never wants to again. Or perhaps he can't bear pipe smokers because "anyone who spends all that time keeping the damn thing lit can't be getting anything worthwhile done."

There is a point of diminishing returns, however, when the specifications become too limited to be practical. If a client believes he must have a Baker Scholar with a CPA and Cleveland-area experience in the metal-working industry, he may find no ethical recruiter will handle the search. A proficient recruiter won't play "yes man" to the client, since he is being paid for his objectivity and expertise.

As a final step in establishing the preliminary relationship, the client can expect both verbal and written feedback from the search consultant. Verbally, they should agree that the particular search is within the consultant's professional scope in terms of level, function, feasibility of specifications and workload.

As a professional, the recruiter will be unwilling to guarantee results, but he should refuse to accept any assignment where the probability of success is dubious. His primary considerations will be long range: turning in a performance that will lead to repeat business, as well as enhancing his reputation in general.

Perhaps the recruiter will say at this point (if he hasn't already) that he is in some degree "blocked" in the client's industry. (This happens when a consultant is already working for a number of competitors; no ethical recruiter attracts individuals from client organizations.) If the client's opening requires specific, technical industrial experience, this prohibition may preclude effective search work. But if the position under discussion involves easily transferable skills—where functional expertise is paramount—effective managers can be attracted across industry lines.

Written feedback from the initial meeting usually arrives at the client's desk looking suspiciously like a form letter. Despite its somewhat dry tone, the letter should cover such areas of possible confusion as projected timetables, professional fees and just which search personnel will handle the assignment. Along with written specifications (usually enclosed, developed from the on-site visit) the letter deserves close attention. Approval of the letter by the client signals that the preliminary communication was productive and that actual work can begin.

THE SEARCH PROCESS

Once the search is in motion, the primary responsibility for continuing the initial productive dialogue belongs to the recruiter. If the client's only communication from the search firm is the monthly bill, he has a right to be irritated. He also can legitimately expect that the senior, or "co-responsible" associate (if there is one), will be informed enough to answer all but the most detailed questions if the assigned consultant is unavailable.

Barring any major difficulties during this stage of the search, a weekly telephone call between the two parties is sufficient. A case in point:

A midwestern manufacturing company, unused to working with recruiters, hired an executive search firm from a major city nearby. Specifications were agreed upon quickly, and the confident client devoted no more attention to the search in the ensuing three months than to pay promptly the consultant's invoices.

At the end of three months, the search executive called to advise that the agreed-upon compensation for the job to be filled was inadequate, and despite his contact with several hundred individuals, he had been unable to interest anyone of the required age, education and experience in the opportunity offered at the stated figure.

While the consultant probably should have had close enough familiarity with the function and industry to question the compensation initially, at the very least he should have advised the client of his difficulties within a matter of weeks, so that an adjustment in specifications could be made.

Unfortunately, by the time the client was able to make the decision to offer greater compensation, the search was already "shopworn"; many of those who would have been attractive candidates had already closed their minds to the position and would be unlikely to renew enthusiasm upon a second contact.

The client did manage to hire an individual some nine months after the assignment had been initiated, but he was never satisfied that many better candidates did not exist. And after that experience, when working with other recruiters, he never let a week go by without picking up the telephone if he had received no word.

Of course, the crime of insufficient compensation is committed by both sides. Another case in point:

A New York-based consultant accepted an assignment from a large business services organization to identify a vice president, marketing for the company's eastern division. Because the client insisted that the need was acute, the consultant brought his firm's talents to bear in the shortest possible time. Within a week, sufficient research had been conducted to allow his recruiters to set up a travel schedule that included personal interviews with four very attractive prospects in Chicago, St. Louis, Minneapolis and San Francisco.

Having already seen three others in New York, he called to give his client a progress report. His enthusiasm was quickly dampened. "Oh, didn't I call you?" responded the client to his news. "We decided the first of this week to promote our midwest man after all. We've already circulated our internal announcement of his promotion."

It's plain to see from the above that both client and consultant have a responsibility to communicate promptly any departure from the agreed-upon plan.

DON'T COMPETE WITH YOUR SEARCH FIRM

One trap the client organization and the recruiter can fall into during this phase is that of competing with each other. For instance, if the client hears of an executive who might fit the search, he benefits by letting the recruiter know. The recruiter can determine the extent of the individual's interest, and eventually help attract him to the opportunity if that course appears advisable. Not telling the recruiter about the candidate jeopardizes the search's stated objective of finding the best executive for the job, and because of recruiting's fee structure, may not save money either.

It also muddies the water to use more than one search firm on the same assignment. Consider the case of Don Smith, an outstanding engineer who is somewhat dissatisfied with his rate of progress. Through different sources, word of his discontent reaches both Recruiter A and Recruiter B, and each one contacts Smith for the same job at Engineers, Inc. Smith's reaction to Recruiter A is positive, but when he hears from Recruiter B, his correct evaluation is that the client is not only inefficient but desperate, and it would be best to keep clear of the situation.

At this time, providing the client is kept informed, he should in turn let the recruiter do his job without undue interference. Attempting to apply pressure to speed the consultant's work will only cause him delay.

Communication prior to the actual interview stage of the search is formalized by means of written evaluations of the few individuals deemed appropriate by the recruiter. Most clients prefer to have all candidates presented at the same time, in order to make the scheduling of interviews and evaluating candidates easier. The alternative, or "shotgun" method of firing off presentations one by one as the recruiter prepares them, tends to make decision making harder despite its seeming contribution of speed.

Although presentations represent many weeks worth of professional time and thought on the recruiter's part, the client should not hesitate to speak up if he feels he has not received adequate information for his decision. Before calling the recruiter on the rug, however, he should determine exactly *why* the report is weak. For instance, is the experience section sufficiently detailed? What personal qualities have made the candidate successful in the past? Why would he or she fit the client opportunity? The company?

INTERVIEWING AND HIRING

During most of the search to this point, the more active role is the consultant's, but during the final stage, the other half of the team, the client, assumes an increasingly important part.

Following the presentation of candidates, the consultant takes a more visible stance as middleman. Although he is still working for the client organization, he has an ethical responsibility to the individual also, and will be more valuable to the client if he maintains this objective middle ground. Providing he is convinced the match is right, the consultant can play a role in keeping client and candidate from prematurely saying no to each other.

If the client is not experienced at interviewing, he should seek, and the consultant should provide, coaching to enhance his effectiveness. Additionally, there are some procedures inherent in the interviewing process that the client should consider. He should:

1. Arrange interviews *quickly* once he has decided to see a candidate. More good executives have lost interest through delay by the client than recruiters care to remember. Even though the interviewer may be busy, he will find interviewing promptly assures a smaller expenditure of his time on the search project in the long run.

2. Take time prior to the interview to become familiar with the individual's background. In this way, during the interview itself, he will be able to devote most of his attention to assessing the critical areas of personal chemistry. Further, his obvious efforts at preparation will strike a favorable chord in the candidate and maintain his interest in pursuing the opportunity.

3. Remember that the candidate did not seek the job, the job sought him. One client turned off his most attractive prospect by asking, "And why did you apply for this position?" instead of selling him on the opportunity.

4. Relay impressions to the consultant as soon as possible after seeing a candidate. The final choice is the client's, of course, but if there were any unanswered questions left dangling, the consultant may be able to settle them with the candidate away from the pressure of an interview.

5. Make a friend for the company. If the personal chemistry isn't right, and the candidate is of no further interest, it's nevertheless good business policy to make the best impression possible. Today's rejected candidate may be tomorrow's customer, competitor or even state senator. The search consultant appreciates the candidate's departing with positive feelings, since he will look favorably on the recruiting industry as a consequence.

After the interview, the consultant will most likely hold a post-mortem with the candidate. Even if the client decided not to pursue this particular executive, the candidate's impressions will be valuable input for future interviews.

REFERENCE CHECKING

Once a definite degree of interest has been established, the client can expect the recruiter to begin a thorough job of reference checking. In this case particularly, the client should be wary of endangering the candidate's job by doing any investigation himself. In one instance, a client was unsure why a candidate was interested in leaving his present employer, and took it upon himself to call the candidate's

One of the most valuable skills of an executive search consultant is his ability to uncover the truth by reference checking a candidate. He'll probably put a lot of time into face-to-face and telephone reference checking. A skilled reference checker can draw extensive meaning from even the briefest conversation, not only from what is said but from how it is said.

chief executive officer rather than allowing the search consultant to make discreet inquiries. Sadly, the candidate was fired within twenty-four hours for his "disloyalty" in considering another employer.

Occasionally, clients comment that reference reports tend to be too favorable. Certainly, any client has a right to know both positive and negative sides of the story. If he does not get them, he should ask that the recruiter dig further. The presence of negatives in a candidate's background does not mean he or she will not fit the job at hand. Most successful people have idiosyncrasies, and it's a question of knowing them and assessing their probable impact on the opportunity under consideration.

After all the information has been submitted, the search moves completely within the client's bailiwick. Procrastination in making a decision only delays the day when the client's management team becomes more effective. A possibly apocryphal story among recruiters tells of the client who, after interviewing two candidates three times apiece, decided between them by tossing a coin. A flippant solution, perhaps, but at least he recognized that point when a decision is necessary.

In search, decisiveness proceeds from trust and a healthy working relationship between client and recruiter. First-time clients are prone to ask, "Don't you think there might be someone else we should see before deciding?" If the recruiter did, he would have searched for and presented the additional candidate. After all, the recruiter wants a satisfied client, repeat business and enhancement of his firm's reputation.

Should the client desire, the consultant will aid in the salary negotiations. He can approach the candidate with a preliminary figure, and he can later act as a liaison should the bargaining process become a complicated one. However, the recruiter usually prefers that the client discuss directly with the candidate fine points of the salary package once it has been agreed upon in general terms.

Success in executive search can come only as the consequence of a true team effort between client and consultant. It is up to the consultant to identify individuals who can do the job, and it is up to the client to hire one who is so qualified without undue delay.

In the process of executive search, sometimes the client acts as coach and the consultant as player. At other times the roles are reversed. However, if both parties contribute their best effort in

An important part of the executive recruiter's job is to brief company executives before they interview a job candidate—and to brief the job candidate before he is interviewed by the company.

either capacity, all participants—client, consultant and candidates—will come out winners in the end.

CHECK LIST FOR THE CLIENT–CONSULTANT TEAM

The client should:

- Meet the search executive who will actually handle the assignment, not just a senior representative of the consulting firm.

- Make certain that the search consultant reports directly to the client representative who has the basic responsibility for selecting the successful candidate. Usually, this is the individual to whom the position reports.

- Take sufficient time to assure that the search consultant understands the company's philosophy and management style.

- Remove the element of surprise, telling the consultant of all pertinent pluses and minuses regarding the company and the position to be filled.

- Remain available to the consultant to answer questions as they arise.

- Set up appointments with candidates promptly, and see that candidates are treated with respect and courtesy.

- Be decisive in evaluating candidates, and extend a reasonable offer once a preference has been established.

In turn, the search consultant should:

- Offer counsel regarding client specifications at the outset, to assure the assignment will be workable.

- Admit his lack of confidence in completing the assignment successfully, should this exist.

- Familiarize the client with the search process, including a detailed description in writing of financial arrangements, the anticipated schedule and personnel involved.

- Respect the confidentiality of client information.

- Maintain communications with the client throughout the search.

- Submit in writing complete background information on candidates, including in-depth reference checking and the consultant's personal evaluation of the individual's suitability to the position.

- Counsel the client (if he so desires) on interviewing, appraising and negotiating with candidates.

THE CASE OF THE RELUCTANT CLIENT

Almost inevitably, stereotyped images and common misconceptions about executive search firms disappear once a competent firm has an opportunity to prove its value.

In one case, the hiring executive in a particular corporation had had a less than satisfactory personal experience with a search consultant. Because of that experience, he decided to avoid the use of a consultant on a key requirement for a division president.

Since confidentiality was not important, he concluded that he would seek suggestions from business associates, his public accountants, legal advisors, and his own staff. This produced a significant number of names, which were subjected to a preliminary screening, and then a handful of apparently qualified candidates were interviewed in depth.

Considerable time was consumed by this process, although a candidate was selected and employed. Prior to the extension of an employment offer, the hiring executive had made a few calls to former employers to effect a "reference check." While all systems were go at the start, within six months severe philosophical differences became apparent, and the recently employed executive resigned to return to his former employer.

Since there were no other candidates from the original effort still available, the hiring executive placed a large newspaper advertisement. The advertisement drew well over one hundred replies. Now, however, he realized he did not have the time to evaluate them appropriately. Finally, he sought the counsel of a search organization.

As the executive described what had happened, he was chagrined to learn that his recently departed executive was well known to the search firm, which quickly identified to him the reasons for the selection error. This insight led the employer to reconsider his original decision to avoid the use

When a company has identified the candidate considered best qualified to fill the job, it is wise to close the deal quickly. The search consultant has an important role to play in bringing about a fast, smooth, mutually satisfactory agreement. Experience proves that delay frequently results in the candidate accepting an opportunity elsewhere.

of a consultant. A professional search was begun and resulted in a satisfactory solution to a problem that by then was much more severe than when first discovered.

In another case, a large international company with multiple product lines recognized the failing health of its vice president, international. A careful study was made of potential replacements from within the organization. Due to the organizational structure itself, however, an appropriate training ground had not existed.

Reluctantly, the president concluded that he would be forced to bring in a replacement from outside his company. He decided to assume responsibility personally for the identification of a successor for his vice president, international, and hoped he could avoid the disruption that could occur should word of this pending opening permeate his executive ranks.

He sought the recommendations of two trusted directors. He mentioned his requirement to a close business associate in a competing company. As might be anticipated, few suggestions resulted, and while even those few were not obvious candidates, the president felt compelled to meet with each. Otherwise he risked appearing uninterested in the comments of his own directors.

Most of the people the president did interview did not meet the specifications of the position. Only one of the candidates, had he been interested, might well have been an adequate answer. At this point, several weeks had passed because of the president's busy schedule.

Meanwhile, the declining health of the incumbent became more obvious, and significantly aroused the anxieties of his subordinates. This further impaired the effectiveness of the total international group. With considerable reluctance, the president then discussed the situation with his vice president, personnel, who in turn sensed the urgency in the situation. It was his strong recommendation that the president not lower his standards, but rather that a competent and experienced consultant be retained to develop a group of both qualified and interested candidates. By good fortune alone, he was able to identify a consulting organization that had recently conducted a search for a similar position. Thus the client was soon able to consider competent internationalists.

During the search firm's discussions with a pair of candidates who were attractive, but from a different industry, the search consultant was able to identify two additional candidates from within the appropriate industry. From this group of four, a suitable candidate to replace the failing vice president, international was found.

6

Reaching the Employment Agreement

Once you have decided on the candidate you want to fill that top-level executive position, you are ready to start working out an employment agreement. You would be well advised not to put off negotiations once the selection has been made; procrastination can be risky. Many good candidates have been lost because the company wanted to interview a few more people, just in case another one might be even better. Sometimes, too, a discussion of terms will be put off for a few weeks because of busy schedules or vacations.

Both recruiter and client should keep in mind that if a candidate is willing to talk to one recruiter, and to you, he may also be talking to others. Sometimes a candidate will use another company's interest in his talents as leverage with his present employer. By stating or hinting that he's been approached, he may be able to gain a promotion, salary increase or whatever, and take himself off the employment market.

In one instance, a communications company put off making a firm offer to a very interested vice presidential candidate for a matter of weeks. By the time the offer was made, the candidate had learned of organizational changes in his present company that netted him a major promotion. He had been prepared to accept the offer originally, but the delay caused him to take the promotion and stay with his present firm.

SELLING YOUR STAFF ON THE NEW EXECUTIVE

Another stumbling block in the preagreement stages can be a lack of cohesion among the management team of the potential employer. When you select the candidate who fits your needs, be sure all the executives involved realize the importance of filling this job and attracting this man to it. Everyone should concur on both the need and the man. The executive search firm can help to stress this point to a client's management staff, pointing out that the company has come to the candidate, not the other way around. The company's attitude should be a positive one. The importance of enthusiasm on the part of your management team, and their interest in the company and the candidate, cannot be emphasized too much.

If, as in one recent example, one key executive is not in agreement, or takes a negative attitude toward the candidate, you may well lose a good potential executive. In this particular case, the company's chief executive officer and other top staff had interviewed and been impressed with the candidate, a feeling that was mutual. The candidate then met alone with the man who would be his group vice president. The vice president said that the job and salary in question would be reviewed soon and that he personally thought the candidate was being offered more money than the job was worth. The candidate felt that he was not wanted by this man, and decided against going with the company.

This kind of problem can be avoided by knowing your own team and putting across how critical it is that they act like a team in the interest of attracting new members of the highest quality.

NEGOTIATING THE EMPLOYMENT AGREEMENT

When the interviewing is done and you and your candidate are in general agreement about the job, negotiations for an employment agreement begin. The executive search consultant can and should play an important role in these negotiations. His knowledge of both company and candidate can be valuable in helping to bring about an agreement that is fair and reasonable in the eyes of both sides.

Also, the search consultant has probably had more experience in developing employment agreements than either of the parties involved. He knows the areas to cover before closing a deal. He is also an objective third party, able to work out compromises or bring the two sides together at any sticky points in the negotiations.

If a company is out of line on, for instance, the salary they are willing to offer, the search firm is familiar enough with the industry to offer advice. One company was considering a $60,000 salary for a vice presidential position; the search firm said its experience indicated that the type of candidate desired would not accept that particular job for less than $75,000. The company made its own checks, agreed, and set $75,000 as its salary target.

Reaching an agreement on terms is the most important factor in negotiations, whether between two nations, management and labor, salesman and customer or management and prospective employee. All previous discussions and good feelings are meaningless unless the parties can come to terms—and that means specifics.

THE COMPENSATION PACKAGE

Preparing the package to offer a candidate is often very delicate and difficult for a company. The package must be sufficiently attractive to win the candidate's acceptance, but it must also be within the boundaries of the company's internal compensation and organizational structure. The salary range must be in line with what the company can afford and what is being given to comparable executives already employed.

The search consultant's broad experience in preparing such packages can be most helpful to a client company that wishes to be fair and reasonable but simply lacks experience in this area. The consultant also has in-depth knowledge of the candidate, his background and what is important to him. The consultant is able to tally this with what is being offered for comparable positions in similar companies. It is the search consultant's responsibility to know the market and to know what it takes to entice a particular individual to change jobs and perhaps move his family. The crucial attractions will vary from one executive to another, and the search consultant will usually have investigated what factors, for instance, are causing the executive to consider leaving his current job. The search consultant will try to determine whether a candidate will take a position if offered, and on what terms. If the terms are plausible, they will be communicated to the company to be included in negotiations.

Search firms have found certain areas to be of concern to most executive candidates. Assuring that these areas are discussed in full,

Assuming a candidate already has a secure job, he'll probably think long and hard about the advantages and disadvantages of accepting a new position even if the compensation package represents a substantial increase. If the new job means moving to a high-cost area, he may decide the raise alone isn't worth it.

at some point in the negotiations, and also in the resulting employment agreement, will help smooth the path for a sound and ungrudging relationship.

Opportunity for Promotion. This is probably the number one concern for the greatest number of candidates. Often a well-paid executive will be dissatisfied with his present job because he doesn't see any place to advance. If you can offer opportunities for promotion—making it apparent without making any promises—this point can make all the difference in attracting top management people.

Attractive Working Environment. Various factors make up a company's working environment, and if it is attractive, this makes a good selling point for executive candidates. A company with low executive turnover, sound financial position and a good reputation for quality and performance in its field will usually attract quality executives. An executive who is already employed in your industry will be aware of your company's image, and if that image is not the best, you may have to offer more in the way of salary, for instance, to compensate. Your candidate will know whether your executives have a reputation for being stimulating and challenging, and what your company philosophy is. And if you and your executive staff are obviously excited about and involved in the firm, this can and should be communicated to the candidate.

Base Salary. While salary is not, surprisingly enough, the first consideration of most executive candidates, it is nonetheless very important. Usually a key employee will not move for less than a 20 per cent increase in his current salary. If he is being asked to move to an expensive metropolitan area such as New York or Chicago, he may want even more. Factors such as the need for seasonal wardrobes, private schools or the prevalence of higher property taxes ought to be figured into salary. An executive coming from a small town in Texas to New York will probably need a larger salary increase to maintain his standard of living. Any executive will certainly expect to be able to live in a style at least comparable to his current one, and to earn a salary competitive with similar positions in the industry and within the individual organizational structure.

Salary can be a difficult area to resolve, and the executive search consultant can often be an effective intermediary between the two parties. A third party provides to each of the participants a knowledgeable outsider with whom to discuss their positions. You want to avoid saying "That's my final offer," until all possibilities have been explored.

Negotiations are serious business, and it's risky to approach them too lightly or unprofessionaly. In one recent case, a search firm was asked to find a scientist for a specialized position in industry. A highly respected man in the field was found, he showed great interest in the position, and the company was most anxious to hire him. The search firm informed the client company that the man was currently earning $40,000, and suggested an offer of at least $50,000 would be needed to get him to take the job.

The vice president in charge of research, however, wanted to be a negotiator. He made the man an offer of $40,000, although he was perfectly prepared to go higher after he'd had the satisfaction of negotiating. The scientist interpreted this attitude to mean he was wasting his time, however, and walked out on the discussions. Although the company tried, it was unable to convince him to talk again. A valuable and prestigious addition to the staff was lost because of an avoidable failure in negotiations.

Total Compensation Package. For senior management, the total package should offer some types of compensation other than salary. An executive earning under $50,000 will probably not be able to consider having some of his income deferred, but most top executives want incentive bonuses, options, tax shelters or some type of compensation that permits estate building. Others look for a system of performance bonuses or similar cash rewards.

With the high cost of medical care today, executive candidates expect a well-executed benefit package covering major medical, surgical, etc. An increasing number of companies are also offering dental insurance. A group life insurance plan, with benefits equal to three to five times base salary, is fairly common. For an employee with a large family, these benefits can be very significant in the choice he makes.

Then, of course, there is the subject of a car, club membership or other perquisites.

In all of these matters, the search counselor can provide assistance. As an objective outsider with experience in evaluating benefits, he can help the company to develop, and the individual to select, the best compensation package for all concerned.

Title. When an individual is changing positions, he is usually concerned about receiving a title that reflects responsibility equal to, or greater than, his last position. Regardless of financial consideration, a company would be wise not to overlook this seemingly small point. There is at least a little ego in all of us.

Reporting Relationship. The candidate usually wants to have a concise understanding of where his position fits into the organizational structure—to whom he reports and who reports to him. During the interviewing stages of negotiations, it will be helpful for all concerned if the candidate meets at some length with the people with whom he will be associated.

In the final selection process, the individual's competence is not usually at issue, but both client and candidate will want to be sure he'll mix well in the corporate environment.

In developing a total package to offer a candidate, all the previous points are fairly basic. But most top-level executives will also have certain individual options that they will want in terms of the job or the compensation. The search consultant can, in his position as intermediary, learn what the executive wants and communicate it to the client company so a package that reflects his wishes can be prepared.

Some top-level executives are very specific about what kind of offer it will take to make them change jobs. If a man is valuable enough, or specialized enough, a company may be prepared to meet detailed demands. In any event, you must be sure of how much you want this candidate and how much of an incentive you are willing to offer to get him to leave his current position and accept yours.

Remember that most executive job candidates are gainfully employed. While it is legitimate to ask a candidate why he is willing to consider leaving his present job, keep in mind that you have come looking for him. He has not come to you for the job.

At this stage of negotiations, you have checked the candidate's background carefully and you obviously believe he will be a valuable addition to your company. Now you must determine how much you are willing to offer to get him on the team. Even an unemployed candidate should be handled with care. Frequently today, mergers and changes in top management can put high-quality executives on the job market. They are still experienced, desirable management talent, and probably won't be out of work long. It would be a mistake to treat them otherwise.

PUT IT IN WRITING

When you have agreed on terms of employment, it's best to put it in writing as a protection for both sides. You may or may not have a formal contract, but you still want to be sure there are no misunderstandings.

Many companies will write a letter to the executive spelling out everything discussed—job specifications, base salary, reporting relationships, benefits, moving costs, etc. The executive will then reply, either by telephone or in writing, and the deal will be settled. Getting it on paper is important though—deals have been known to fall through between the spoken agreement and the written one.

Whether or not you have a contract is generally a matter of

individual company policy; some companies standardly use them; others never do. In some cases, an executive will request a contract of a company that does not generally make use of them. Then the search consultant can again act as intermediary, testing the company's willingness to consider a contract and discovering how badly—and why—the executive wants one. One company, in a recent example, wanted a particular executive badly enough to go along with his wishes and change its no-contract policy. They not only wrote a contract for the new employee but for the other executives at the same or higher level in the organization.

An executive does take a risk when he moves from one company to another and a contract gives him some security. Some companies, recognizing this, will sign a letter of intent. This grants a year's salary if the employment should be terminated within the first year. It is, in a sense, a two-year contract.

Whether the contract is formal or not, remember that you want to keep your new executive happy once he gets into the office. Making him part of the company family, taking him to lunch and showing him around will help to make him comfortable in his new environment. If you have found him to be desirable executive talent, others probably have too, so you want to get him off to a good and satisfying start in your organization.

This doesn't mean kowtowing to the new man, but it does mean helping him to make a smooth adjustment.

One new executive with a major multinational firm was given a few weeks to get his feet on the ground and many opportunities to get to know the organization. Within six weeks, he had adjusted and was busy working on major assignments, and very happy. The company made a real effort to make him part of the team, and all concerned were quickly able to see the results.

THE CASE OF THE HESITANT EXECUTIVE

Management must understand the importance of timing throughout an executive search. Often, there is a crucial moment when an attractive candidate's attitude vacillates between excitement for a tantalizing new position and complacency with his present job. Striking while the iron is hot can be of critical consequence.

For example, take the case of the plant manager of a large midwestern manufacturing company. It was determined that a new position of group vice president needed to be created. It became apparent to management that they would have to look outside the organization to find a qualified candidate.

The company also was interested in hiring the best candidate available. The company told the search firm it consulted for the assignment, "Let's not rush it. Let's be sure."

During the months that followed, several highly qualified candidates were interviewed. The president of the company agreed with the search consultant that the candidates had 95 per cent of the qualifications but added, "Let's continue our search to see if we can do better."

Several months passed and after interviewing additional candidates, the president decided he would like to make an offer to the second man he'd interviewed. That interview, however, had taken place over three months ago.

After his initial interview three months ago, the particular candidate had correctly concluded that the company was going to continue its search because he had not heard anything in the interim. At the same time, he had let his superior know that he'd had a very interesting interview with one of the company's chief competitors.

The man's superior, apparently sensing he risked losing a highly valuable employee, acted quickly. Later, when the executive search recruiter again contacted the candidate, he was surprised to find him no longer interested in the new group vice presidency.

The candidate had been made group vice president within his own company, receiving a substantial increase in salary and bonus, a company car and free membership in a country club.

Reaching the employment agreement with a candidate is what executive search is all about. All of the efforts that go into searching for a candidate are meaningless unless you come to an agreement and the candidate is placed on the payroll. Timing is of the essence.

In another case, a highly qualified candidate balked in the final stages of the employment agreement talks when he sensed he was not being told the true specifications of his new assignment.

The company's search firm had succeeded in identifying a new plant purchasing agent for one of the company's subsidiaries. The general plant manager, however, who had initiated the request for a new plant purchasing agent, had failed to inform his staff that he was actually going to reorganize the operation. Furthermore, the new man was actually going to take on a new and expanded role as manager of materials management.

Consequently, when the candidate requested an opportunity to meet and talk briefly with some of the managers who would be working at his level, he heard some startling things.

The managers, unaware of the pending reorganization, told the candidate they thought he was extremely overqualified for the simple position of plant purchasing agent.

The result was that the candidate turned down the offer, as he felt he was not being told the true specifications of the new assignment.

7
The Transition

Having gone through the trauma of continuous interviews, you have nominated a successful candidate. He has climbed the first hill, but the sheer cliff of reality stands before him. What does he do now? How does he arrange his movements? What of his family, his obligations? Countless other questions now face him as the successful candidate.

One executive who has moved several times for major corporations stresses that first of all you must let your successful candidate take a breather. Don't try to rush him into his new assignment. Although the demands at this time seem to point toward immediate and new corporate immersion, bear in mind that the disturbance to his family is even greater than the disturbance that may exist for him personally.

DON'T RUSH IT

There are some instances where companies have urged the new executive to take at least thirty days holiday before reporting for his new assignment. This takes some of the edge off the tension that accrues with the changing of jobs. Nothing puts a man in better shape than to report to work after a good rest.

Like business itself, executive search has become a worldwide activity. The best candidate for a particular job may now be located in some remote business capital.

Certainly, ninety to one hundred twenty days is good timing for the movement to the new assignment. To a degree, this is the same traumatic experience as a divorce and remarriage, and the chances are that the new executive's family will feel much the same way. The tying together of loose ends, both in personal planning and closing down the present home, are things that a wife and family usually consider to be, emotionally, extremely important.

From the standpoint of the children, what are the schools like in comparison with those they are leaving? If the move is within the United States, it is a good idea to have the new executive have his children do some exploring as to the type of school system they will be facing. Have him inquire what curriculum is offered. Ask him to be mindful that it ties in with their existing education. Suggest that he let the children themselves do the writing as this will draw them into the move and make them feel they are participating. It eliminates, for the children, as much as possible, the voids that occur in this experience.

One word of caution should be projected and that is the necessity of having your head of employee relations involved in facilitating tying loose ends together. There are all kinds of last minute decisions to be made on the part of the corporation. The head of employee relations should be empowered to make these decisions, obviously with a limitation as to costs. This eliminates additional wear and tear on the new executive after the "matchmaking" has occurred.

FIRST-HAND VISITS

Be aware that the moving family must have the opportunity to examine the new environment first-hand. By no means should the employing corporation be niggardly in providing accommodations and transportation in order to achieve this perspective. This is where the family will live, making their contribution to the new community as well as to your company.

It is at this point that your corporation can win the lasting respect of the new executive. This is the time when the attitude of the new executive and his family toward the company will be formed. It is paramount that someone in a senior capacity be at the airport or depot to meet, greet and put at ease the new candidate's wife and children.

Prior to his arrival, inquiry should have been made as to housing needs and requirements. Everything should be done to demonstrate the sincerity of interest in his problems.

Certainly, luncheons, dinners and get-togethers with bankers, influential club members and community leaders can more quickly assist the family and new executive in adjusting. From a corporate standpoint, albeit selfishly, the sooner and more intelligently you lay his problems to rest, the sooner he can be called upon to contribute and advance his interest in the company.

In one instance, a company president invited a new executive to attend a briefing that the president was giving to the investment community in San Francisco. This allowed the new executive to not only become acquainted with the attitudes of the company as expressed by the presentation, but also to ensure that his introduction to the investment community was on a proper basis.

Assuming the new executive has moved to a new location for his job with you, it is wise to encourage frequent visits from his wife, if only to resolve the problem of housing. Also, he should be prodded to return to his family from time to time prior to their arrival at the new location in order to allay their anxieties.

Remember, this is not only the hiring of an individual, but of a family, with all of its complexities.

THE COST OF TRANSITION

Who pays for it all? You as the hiring company. Now is not the time to squeeze. It should be delicately imparted to this new executive that he should recognize that the company with which he is now associated is generous. There should be an open awareness that your company wishes to have him adapt and relocate as easily as he can, but that a two-way street does exist. Now is the time to observe how much the new executive draws on his "goodwill credit line."

His children are in private school. It is perfectly normal for a corporation to reimburse the new executive coming on board for tuition paid for private education; for the disposal of his home at no loss to him (based on the end appraisal); living cost basis; the settlement of household leases and such types of commitments made by the transferee.

Is the new executive's yacht allowable? That depends on the position offered. If the position is that of a key executive, a boat could be transferred—if it falls in the plus or minus 38-foot category. His automobiles also could be considered normal ticket items, usually limited to two. For the equestrian-minded family, you can fairly state that horses are taboo. The primary desire is to make possible the "hold-harmless" situation for the new key executive.

It is absolutely essential that both parties should acknowledge agreement on all points. Nothing can erode confidence on both sides more quickly than the feeling that understandings reached have not been honored. No one should take umbrage at the need for written agreements.

DISCOURAGE "TRANSFERRED" FILES

You hired him. He seems knowledgeable. At the onset there should be complete harmony in that he is expected to contribute freely his know-how. A word of advice: It is wise to discourage any accompanying files. They are not your specifics. Remember that integrity works both ways. The man who moves in with a filing cabinet is viewed with uncertainty as to his ethical qualifications. Major corporations do not operate, nor should *any* corporation operate, on an espionage basis.

During the first six months, the new executive should have frequent exposure to the individual in the company who did most of the negotiation in his hiring. This allows a graceful course of continuing indoctrination, and helps to keep the new executive informed as to his progress and his general acceptance by his peers. It also gives the new executive the opportunity to raise questions on an informal basis, and such contact can act as an escape valve for some of his frustrations that may arise.

THE THREE-YEAR ADJUSTMENT

The executive has made his move, his children are in school, all claims for moving have been paid and he is on the job. His first six months have passed and the adjustment to the new corporation has been made. However, bear in mind that the real adjustment takes up to three years before you can really say that it has been fully accomplished. More executives have left jobs between the second and third years than at any other time during their adjustment period. Therefore, since recruiting a good executive is both expensive and disturbing to your company, you should by all means keep working to keep him happy and "on board." This does not mean pampering but rather a steady exposure and a good understanding, bearing in mind that good management, although not listed on the balance sheet, is one of the best assets that any corporation can have.

THE CASE OF THE TRAUMATIC TRANSITION

The need for adroit handling of a high-level recruitment does not end when the selected candidate agrees to take the job. Professional search consultants realize that there may be serious complications in the process of actually moving from the previous company to the new one, and they offer expert counsel to their clients to forestall last-minute difficulties that may get the relationship off to a sour start or even abort it at the point of inception. Here is a case in point.

When Gorgon Manufacturing of Chicago needed a new vice president of marketing, the company's president, Andrew Turner, decided that the job was important enough to warrant his handling it himself. Dispensing with the services of a search consultant, Turner undertook the recruitment project personally.

Turner's efforts took considerable time, but he felt that it had paid off when he was able to hire George Randall. Randall had been marketing director for a Hartford company whose business was similar to Gorgon's but not in competition with it.

It happened that Gorgon had scheduled a series of regional meetings to begin on the Monday following Randall's last day with his old employer. Andrew Turner felt that this situation presented an ideal opportunity for Randall to become acquainted quickly with the Gorgon sales organization. The president arranged for the new head of marketing to join the company at the site of the eastern regional meeting in New York on his first day in the new job.

The search had taken a lot of Turner's time, and he now concentrated on other important matters. George Randall came to the meeting in New York without having received an agenda. At this meeting Randall would be introduced to the vice president of sales, whom he had not met previously.

The New York meeting ended on Thursday. Randall went on to Chicago, where he spent Friday getting acquainted with some of his new associates. On Sunday he left for Atlanta—along with the vice president of sales—to attend the southeast regional meeting. From Atlanta, Randall would move on to meetings in Houston, Denver, Los Angeles and Seattle. He followed this routine for four weeks, spending the third weekend with his family in Hartford.

The tight schedule had given George Randall only a day and a half to look for a house in the Chicago area. Time had not permitted him to bring his wife out to join him.

At the end of five weeks of almost constant travel, Randall was able to take a few days off. Mrs. Randall joined him in Chicago to look for a suitable place to live. Not surprisingly, she had become increasingly impatient at the delay.

One obvious requirement for the Randall's new home was that it be easily accessible by commuter railroad. Then, of course, there were the factors of schools, type of community, the right sort of house, and so forth. Mrs. Randall felt, reasonably enough, that in a suburban area as large as that surrounding Chicago she should have at least a full week to look around. However, company policy allowed only four days, including a weekend. No exception was made because of Randall's senior position. Andrew Turner might have cut through the difficulties, but by this time he was on a trip to London, Paris and Dusseldorf.

Mrs. Randall had not been very happy about moving from Hartford in the first place. For one thing, although the president of Gorgon had met her, it had been strictly a pro forma meeting. Turner had never discussed the job with her, let alone any of the problems of moving and relocation that were uppermost in her mind. During her several nights in Chicago the president was away. The president's wife had not communicated with Mrs. Randall at all.

By the time Mrs. Randall returned to Hartford she had made up her mind that *nothing* would make her move to Chicago.

During the next six weeks George Randall struggled with the dual tasks of orienting himself to his new responsibilities and trying to persuade his wife to relent. Beset by his personal distractions, he was having great difficulty in getting into the swing of things at Gorgon. He had no luck with the latter effort either; Mrs. Randall became progressively more negative. No amount of urging could convince her that she was welcome in Chicago.

Finally, to save his marriage, George Randall resigned. His career was now in jeopardy. Moreover, Gorgon Mfg. had by now wasted nearly a year without having a key position filled by a talented executive—and the whole task of recruitment had to be resumed.

8
The Candidate's Role in a Successful Executive Search

By Robert W. Lear

When an executive recruiter accepts an executive search assignment, he also accepts the responsibility for presenting to his client, and verifying, an effective amount of factual quantitative data and reliable qualitative observations about each candidate he presents at the employment altar.

All recruiters understand this, but some do a far superior job than others in carrying it out.

By the same token, however, when a candidate accepts an invitation to participate in this delicately balanced game, he should also recognize that he has a few responsible duties to perform, which are critical to a successful culmination of the search. To put it another way, if he fails to measure up to certain expected standards, he will jeopardize his own chances of being chosen and will absolutely make the search more difficult for both the client and the recruiting firm.

Not all candidates understand this, and not all recruiters do a thorough job of explaining these responsibilities to their prospective candidates. The inevitable result is an inordinate number of irritated and frustrated clients, messed-up interviews, and ineffective or busted searches—an unrewarding activity in which everybody loses.

Therefore, it is quite appropriate to see what can be done to encourage recruits to become better candidates, and to get recruiters to take a firmer role in counseling them to do so.

With this objective in mind, here are eight areas for an executive job candidate to be concerned about; he can be certain that the company interviewing him is going to be concerned about them also.

Full, Factual Honesty. Says one company president: "If I catch a candidate head-faking, he's out." What this president means is that if the candidate tries to get away with that "Class of '52" gag when he went to college for only a year, or when he inflates a past title, or when he buries a six-month gap in his employment record, this president assumes the candidate will probably cheat when he comes aboard the new company, too.

The most persistently silly area of obfuscation is in compensation. The candidate ought to lay the facts out cold—complete salary record, specific bonus pay-outs, detailed option situations, exact pension and vesting status, and clearly listed and costed fringes and perquisites. One of the last things an executive employer wants to discuss with a candidate is the details of the future compensation package, but compensation is one of the first things the employer wants to know about the candidate's background.

The candidate simply has to see these things through the client's eyes. The client is used to having verified facts on his in-house candidates. The records are detailed and clear. So, when the stranger is coy about the whole truth, he is going to lose or endanger the sale. Much of the blame for "gaposis" should really rest on the recruiter, for he has to be the intermediary who insists on the detail from the candidate, and then verifies its accuracy.

Preinterview Homework. It takes an alert interviewer about two minutes to find out if a candidate has learned enough about the company to have a successful interview. If the candidate hasn't even read the annual report, chances are he will have a very short session. At the minimum, he should be up to date on the current 10-K and the last quarterly report, have checked Standard & Poor's and found at least one financial analyst's report on the company or the industry. He has to know the basic organization, board composition and major financial and market situations. Unpreparedness before being hired automatically indicates unpreparedness later, too.

On the other hand, creativity and extra effort cost little and produce much. Recently, a candidate walked into an interview, shook hands with the president and said, "Last night I went into two supermarkets and shopped them for your products. I want to ask you some questions." The president was instantly influenced in a positive way.

There may be some situations in which a candidate should be forgiven inadequate preinterview briefing on his own hook, but the recruiter has certainly had enough time to accumulate a small, pertinent library of information and it is his job to see that the candidate sees it—and it's the candidate's job to read it.

Comprehension of the Job. It is astonishing how frequently a candidate misunderstands the scope or structure of the position he is appraising. Sometimes the misunderstanding is caused by poor communication between client, recruiter, and candidate, which is another way of saying sloppy work. Sometimes the recruiter unconsciously oversells the job and sugar-coats the rough edges. Sometimes the candidate, either purposely or through wishful thinking, twists the job to suit his own conception.

This is an expensive waste of time and a source of much disenchantment. The way to minimize it is for the recruiter to fight through a clear understanding of a written job description with the client and with each candidate.

Occasionally this requires a high degree of tact and statesmanship on the part of the recruiter. For example, a company set out to recruit a new president, but left in wishy-washy condition the question of whether or not the president would be the chief executive officer or the chief operating officer. This obviously hampered the recruiter in his search for the ideal candidate. By adroit discussion with the key principals at the client company, the executive recruiter was able to convince them to crystallize the job description so that the candidate could present himself properly.

What it all boils down to is this: Neither the client nor the recruiter wants to put a man in a wrong job any more than the candidate wants it to happen to him. So it's a tripartite affair, with each of three parties responsible for seeing that the understanding of the job is unequivocally clear.

The Reason for Leaving. The question of why the candidate is willing to consider leaving his company and why he has left earlier

jobs is usually the prime time-consumer in recruiting interviews—
and there is probably justification for it. Despite this, when the
question comes, many candidates gag, weasel, blush, orate compul-
sively or in various other ways react poorly.

Much of this messy "spilled-milk" analysis can be avoided if the
candidate establishes proper rapport with the recruiter. The candidate must give the recruiter full disclosure of any important details
surrounding his departure from previous jobs before he meets the
client; otherwise, the recruiter should refuse to represent him. The
recruiter must be able to verify the candidate's story at some stage in
the process and definitely do so before a commitment to hire occurs.

When there are good, positive reasons for leaving an earlier job,
they can be delivered briefly and with candor: "My family hated
Omaha and the job in California was a better one. It gave me a
chance to move into a general managerial post five years ahead of
schedule."

Similarly, just because a candidate has had a blow up at his former
spot need not disqualify him at all. In this case, however, there is all
the more reason for an intimate review between the recruiter and the
candidate—and more attention given as to how the report is to be
made to the client. If it was a personality conflict, explain it. If it was
a competitive situation and our man ran a strong second, say so. If it
was a dismissal for economic reasons, admit it and detail the
reasons—but don't call it a "resignation."

Most company presidents or other interviewers admire a man who
can cope with a job disappointment, face up to it with frankness and
actually benefit from the experience. That's what life is all about.
Even Babe Ruth struck out—1,330 times.

In this category of reference nothing discourages a client faster
than a candidate with a sour grapes attitude towards his present or
former employer. When an interviewee says, in effect, "I worked
for a lousy company and my boss was a fraud," an interviewer will
anticipate that the candidate will carry that same attitude into the
client company. A better explanation would be, "The company was
in trouble. The managers were nice guys, but they couldn't seem to
put the right programs together. I had a great work experience as a
result, but it was wise to leave." The best answer is usually a candid
one.

All of these answers need to be listened to carefully and then checked back through both the obvious and the oblique references. When different stories emerge, it is time to flash the yellow light.

Most clients learn to rely on the recruiter to ferret out half-truths and partial pictures. As for the candidate, the recruiter can be invaluable in authenticating the posture of the client.

Common-sense Courtesy. There's a time-and-place futility connected with outside recruiting. Schedules are terribly difficult to match up and equally hard to keep. No in-house candidate would ever dream of carelessly handling an appointment time or date, but outside candidates seem to think it is cool to play hard-to-get by being unpunctual, unreliable and unavailable. This is fallacious.

Clients respond favorably to the candidate (and the recruiter who so counsels) who says, "Look. We can't seem to find a mutual time this week on our calendars. I'm prepared to meet you for breakfast at 7 a.m. or cocktails at 7 p.m., or at the Admiral's Club in Chicago or I'll come to Scarsdale on Saturday or Sunday."

But the clients are put off by the candidate who strolls in late, keeps switching dates and doesn't return calls in a timely way. The client knows that he is recruiting the *candidate,* but he also believes

Some of the most important steps in the executive search process take place away from the office, particularly in restaurants and airports.

that the job he is offering is a good one and he does not have to demean himself or his company to find the right man. Good managers, good salesmen and good negotiators almost inevitably have good manners when they deal with their counterparts; good candidates should, too.

Unto Thine Ownself Be True. An interview is conducted under forced circumstances at best. As a result, there are times when good personal salesmen have won prizes over all-thumbs candidates who were perhaps better men. Some star producers are taciturn, shirt-sleeved operators who do poorly in a blue suit in a fancy New York City office. How to get the real person to reveal himself to the client can sometimes be a perplexing problem for the recruiter—and, of course, for the candidate.

If habitat is important, then the recruiter and the client should occasionally visit the Mohammedan and see him at ease. Alternatively, they should arrange to have longer interviews or more of them, or properly prepare all parties for a different personality, and then put heavy weight on a double-checked track record of results.

There are doubtless many cases in which the personal dress and customs of the prospective candidate become a matter of great concern to certain clients. It can be a rude shock to a pristine, narrow-tied client when his long-haired candidate appears before him in a double-knit suit with wide lapels and flared pants. Yet, if that's the way the guy normally dresses (and why not?), then it's wrong to fool the client by appearing in a special interview masquerade costume. The better way, perhaps, is for the recruiter to forewarn the client by asking if he has any objection to whatever special mode of dress is coming up—after all, John DeLorean did all right at General Motors. The same candid, preinterview revelation should be made regarding any other personal habit that may differ from the client's expectations, including drinking. These things should be resolved quickly.

In the case of some men and jobs, particularly those at a level below the first corporate tier, more effective client preparation and interviewing often can be done with second-tier client managers rather than with the president. With these people, the candidate is more at ease and more revealing, thus more appraisable. In the case of one company president, he seeks the judgment of his senior personnel officer and one or two key staff officers, and pays particular attention to qualitative personality reactions.

When a top, top job is involved—corporate president, executive vice president or group vice president—the candidate himself has to be mature and cogent enough to look at the negotiation as a two-way street. *He* should be just as interested in seeing that the full personalities of the key client characters are revealed as they are in seeing *his* inner self. As the foreplay works out, then the recruiter should help the client and candidate arrange to see one another in less rigid circumstances—over a weekend, on a golf course, at a lodge, with wives etc. After all, if these men are planning to spend forty hours a week together for several years, a few dry-run companionate hours might make sense for both sides.

A top New York City recruiter tells of a search case that involved the president of a large chemical company and a candidate for the job of vice president, finance. The two men, after appropriate background reviewing and interviewing, were getting along well and a job offer appeared imminent. The client rather suddenly asked the candidate if he would take a psychology test to serve up final proof of forthcoming compatibility. The candidate answered, "I'd be glad to—providing you do it too!" The subject was dropped, the candidate was hired, and he worked out very nicely.

Calling It Off. Just as every candidate is not going to get the job, every candidate is not going to want it. Often, a candidate realizes early in the mating game that he will probably not take the job if offered. Still, he keeps the client on the string for reasons of vanity, chicanery or simply procrastination. Clients hate to be strung along by some guy on an ego trip; candidates demean themselves by such actions.

Again, the recruiter should be the catalyst or the watchdog who forces a reading of the candidate–client blending process. This takes a shrewd and experienced recruiter, for a firmly interested candidate may try to enhance his bargaining power by delaying. It helps a lot if the candidate is told at the outset that he will be pressed for an early *negative* decision.

The worst offender is the man who has been tendered an offer and has given a tentative acceptance. "I think we're okay," he says, but then he adds that he wants to talk with his wife, or a friend or just

Company executives often will interview a candidate jointly, then compare their impressions of what he said and how he handled himself.

wants to "let it jell for a few days." Sometimes this is another way of saying that he's going to go back to his boss and negotiate a raise, using the client and the recruiter as a foil. Sometimes it is the plaint of a man who can't make up his mind. All of the time, if he drags it out too long before he finally declines, he has created extreme discomfort for the client. How to stop candidates from doing this is a difficult problem, but the recruiter should jaw-bone the candidate as to his responsibilities in this area, and should give the client the benefit of his wisdom and experience when he sees signs of this delayed slough-off taking place.

Postinterview Homework. Things have gone well; the client likes the candidate and vice versa; a tentative offer is tendered for appraisal and discussion. At this point, the candidate should be responsible for his last course of action before finally accepting or rejecting. That means doing more homework, but on a higher level.

The candidate should, with whatever degree of freedom he can be granted, begin to talk in greater depth with people within the company, and perhaps with some external sources of information, such as directors, bankers and key figures in the industry. He should read and study in-depth documents, perhaps a few of a confidential nature, supplied by the client. He may wish to bring in his lawyer or accountant.

The point here is that the candidate has a responsibility to himself, and he should satisfy this responsibility before making his final decision. The client and the recruiter should recognize the candidate's responsibility to himself and help him satisfy it. Otherwise the deal may fall through at the threshold.

Consider these words by one company president who has been in the roles of both candidate and client:

> When I look back over my singular experience as a candidate, I believe that both my recruiter and my client did a good job of dealing with me. The search firm knew the client, was aware of the primary and secondary reasons why a recruitment was being undertaken, and properly assessed the emotional make-up of the individuals involved in the selection decision. They prepared me with factual data and with tactful suggestions for approach. They prepared the client for me and encouraged him to work effectively with me as I went about my counter-investigations. As a result, they made the marriage and, as matchmaker, received a substantial and justifiable fee.
>
> What did I learn through my candidacy? A lot, I think.
>
> I am now much more critical and intolerant of an inept, incomplete or inaccurate presentation by a candidate, but I list the recruiting firm as co-defendant. I am now much more demanding of the recruiter for factual double-checking and for candidate counseling. I am now more exacting in my approach to the recruiter and more specific in my interviews with the candidate.
>
> As a result, I'm getting more and better service from recruiters and, most important of all, because I'm a more knowledgeable client, I'm getting better people for my company—and that's the name of the game.

THE CASE OF THE DAZZLER VS. THE DIGGER

A job candidate's "star qualities"—appearance, speaking ability, self-confidence, and so forth—count for a lot. But a good evaluation digs far below the surface and it isn't always the dazzler who gets the job—as this example illustrates.

Bob Connor had been described more than once as being a "superb one-on-one man." Connor had heard the description—and agreed with it. He was proud of his ability to impress and persuade others and to take command of a face-to-face interview.

This gift made Connor an effective salesman. As he moved up the ladder, he adapted his capacities to each new challenge. No question or problem, no matter how unexpected, left him at a loss for words. Since Connor's personal potency was accompanied by nerve and brains, he had grown to become a first-rate marketing executive.

When executive search consultant Ray Perry was given the assignment of finding a marketing vice president for Omnipotent Products, Inc., Connor was one of the first candidates he met with. Like others, Perry was highly impressed with Connor. Connor knew the lunch with the search man had gone well. He was glad; the job at Omnipotent was the kind of plum toward which he had shaped his whole career.

Perry decided that Connor had a very good chance. There were, of course, other candidates. Harold Bayersdorf had a fine track record in marketing. When Perry met Bayersdorf, he formed great respect for Bayersdorf's intellect and his analytical approach to marketing questions. At the same time, the search executive noted that this candidate was not exactly an electric circus as a conversationalist. Bayersdorf liked to think before he spoke. When he talked, his comments were terse and to the point—but not necessarily scintillating.

Both candidates possessed qualities which fitted well with Omnipotent's requirements. Perry arranged for each to meet with Les Wrangel, the chairman and chief executive officer of the giant corporation.

Connor came first. After some preliminaries, Wrangel asked, "What do you know about us?" Connor leaned back and smiled. "I know you're big. I know you're powerful. I know the tremendous scope that your top marketing man would have. There's a lot more I'd like to know." Connor went on to ask some broad questions. The conversation flowed smoothly. Connor emerged from it with great confidence.

When Wrangel asked Bayersdorf that same question, the answer was, "Until four days ago, all I knew was what I read in the papers." Bayersdorf rummaged in his briefcase, pulled out some marked-up copies of articles and of the Omnipotent annual report. "I've done some homework since then, Mr. Wrangel, and there are some things that puzzle me." Bayersdorf went on to ask some sharply angled questions. In one case, Wrangel had to phone his treasurer for an answer. He admitted he did not have the answers to a couple of other questions Bayersdorf asked.

Both candidates wrote follow-up letters. Connor said he had enjoyed their talk and looked forward to their next meeting. Bayersdorf said the same; but he also raised two more questions which had not come up before.

The job went to Bayersdorf. "I liked both of those men," Wrangel told Perry. "But I guess I am inclined to lean toward a guy who really does his homework and is willing to ask tough questions, not just the easy kind that keeps the conversational ball rolling."

9
Executive Search Fees

The reason most prominent corporations use executive search firms is simply that it is profitable to do so.

Time is money to the corporation and to the executives responsible for conducting the search. To put the matter of fees for executive search services in proper perspective, consider how costly of time and money it is for an organization to do the executive recruiting job itself. It has been estimated that a professional recruiter may spend well in excess of two hundred fifty hours to do a normal search; that is, one that does not require unusual qualifications. For a company executive to do the job on his own, he obviously has to spend most of his time on his primary duties and responsibilities, and then devote only part of his time to finding the needed executive. In such cases, the in-house executive search almost always gets short shrift.

In general, it has been estimated that companies attempting to fill key positions on their own spend over twice as much time to complete the job as does the recruiting specialist.

Time is money to the executive recruiting firm, as well as to the client company being served. The searcher's only tangible assets are his experience and available sources of information concerning likely prospects. By devoting 100 per cent of his time to the specialty of recruiting executives, the search consultant can obviously do a better job.

Another big advantage is that clients using professional recruiters are well aware of the cost of searches before they begin. Companies doing the work themselves may never fully know the total hidden drain of time, dollars and energy. Perhaps the most cogent reason to use outside professional recruiting firms is that, doing the recruiting job itself, the company may accept a less-qualified executive simply because it is expedient to do so. A search firm, whose reputation is built on its track record, must consistently deliver highly qualified candidates.

RECRUITERS VERSUS COUNSELORS AND AGENCIES

Frequently executive recruiting consultant firms are confused with employment agencies or career counseling firms. *Fees* are the one important area that immediately distinguishes the professional executive recruiting consultant. As is the case in other professions, his *fees are not contingent* upon completion of an assignment. They are paid on an agreed-upon progressive basis as the search continues, whether or not the assignment is completed.

Another distinguishing feature of the professional recruiter is that *in no instance does an individual become liable to pay a fee*—in whole or in part, directly or indirectly—on account of any service performed.

While fee and billing arrangements may vary among firms, recruiting firms can no more devote the necessary time to the assignment without compensation than can management consultants in other fields. Further, just as there can be no guarantee of a favorable verdict in a law suit, or success in a surgical procedure, there can be no guarantee in a search assignment that an ideal candidate will ultimately be engaged. Therefore, during the course of the search, clients are invoiced monthly for agreed-upon fees, plus out-of-pocket expenses. These monthly installments generally range from one-third to one-fourth of the total fee involved. They are credited toward the total fee when the individual is employed. Usually a final billing for any remaining fee is rendered at that time.

If the candidate is employed at less than the authorized compensation, the final bill will be calculated accordingly, unless a greater amount has already been incurred for work done.

If the search extends beyond the period of time allocated, and the agreed-upon progressive payments have totaled the normal fee, the recruiting firm will usually continue the search on an out-of-pocket-expenses-only basis, unless there are unusual circumstances.

UNUSUAL FEE PRACTICES

As in the case of most professions, fees charged by executive recruiting consultants vary. Generally, however, the following methods are most common.

Method	Comments
Percentage—25 to 35 per cent of first year's guaranteed compensation	Used by the majority of recruiting firms.
Flat amount—a set amount prefixed on basis of estimated time, level of position and difficulty of search	A significant number of firms use this method, if client insists.
Retainer—monthly payments for an agreed-upon period of time	Occasionally used to provide outside counsel to management.
Hourly basis—hourly charges for time recruiter spends in conducting search	Generally available if client prefers charges on this basis.
Per-diem basis—a daily charge for time recruiter spends in conducting search	Rarely used; a few search firms will work on a daily basis if client desires.
Project basis—charge on basis of all costs attributable to search: consultant's time, secretarial assistance, postage, telephone and so forth	A few recruiting firms work solely on this basis.
Minimum fee—lowest charge for a search assignment	Majority of recruiting firms have an established minimum fee, below which they will not work.

Method	Comments
Out-of-pocket expenses— mainly for travel and meals, long-distance telephone calls and other costs relating to the client's assignment	These are generally billed on a monthly basis.
Research—a monthly charge for the research efforts of the recruiting firm	Some consultants bill their research activities separately on a monthly basis.
Billing frequency—invoicing to the client for professional services and expenses	Most popular method is on a monthly basis with a final bill after the client has selected his candidate.

A typical search will take from two to five months on the average. This amount of time is required to do the job well. With the short supply of well-qualified executives, it is possible that in the future this time period will be extended.

The most important thing to remember about the fees of a professional recruiting consultant is that he works only on assignment to find key executives for management—never to find positions for individuals looking for employment. His fee is paid only by the client, and is based on professional services and expenses. Therefore, the professional consultant is never in a position of having to sell candidates to his client. This is the reason he can retain the complete objectivity that makes him a true professional.

← presentation of resumes

10

How to Locate Executive Search Firms

You can let your fingers do the walking and find your executive search firm in the yellow pages only on one condition—you already know the name of the firm you want to look up. Otherwise, your problem is considerably different. For example, a recent edition of the Manhattan yellow pages includes a full page of executive recruiting consultants, loosely defined. At least a dozen of Manhattan's better-known search firms are listed here, together with lesser-known firms, but their names are intermingled with the names of employment agencies, job counselors, research services and other types of firms that fly the executive search banner.

DIRECTORIES

Chances are what you need is an honest-to-goodness directory of search firms, something that you can use like a checklist or memory aid, maybe even something that tells you which firms have offices near you or near your hiring location. Such directories do exist; several are listed at the end of this chapter, along with brief descriptions and advice about their availability. Write to the Association of Executive Recruiting Consultants, Inc. (AERC), 347 Madison Avenue, New York, N. Y. 10017, and request a list of their member firms, as well as a copy of the Association of Consulting Management Engineers (ACME) list of executive recruiting consultants. AERC will send both to you free. They will not serve all your purposes, since many good search firms are not members of AERC or ACME, but these directories are a starting point for you. Some other directories designate the search firms that are AERC members, because these firms have all endorsed common standards of ethical practices. Nonmembership certainly does not imply a lack of ethical standards; some of the top firms have decided not to participate in the association for their own reasons.

PROBLEMS WITH DIRECTORIES

No matter which directory you use, you can depend on it that the information will not be 100 per cent accurate. This is usually not the fault of the publishers; firms change addresses, personnel and ownership. Sometimes they go out of business. Information that was accurate when published may be wrong in a matter of days. What do you do to keep up with changes that may become important to you?

Some companies maintain a "Search Firms" file and add to it all the bits of information that come from various sources. Some of the information you will add to such a file will come by mail directly from the search firms themselves. Most search firms try to keep their client market informed, via brochures and newsletters, notices of additions to their staffs, and the like. Some search firms issue annual reports, not of the financial type, but reports that include photographs of principals and a little horn-tooting about the searches they have completed in the past year, plus routine information about branch office addresses, new departments and maybe some observations about the executive job market as they see it. It can all add up to a fat file of information.

Add to your file by getting acquainted personally with search firm representatives. Invite principals of the firms that interest you to come in and tell you about their firms, their specialty areas of service, their billing arrangements and the qualifications of staff members. Keep notes on what they say, and add your notes to the file. If you become active in assigning searches, you will soon be getting calls from various search firms; most are alert to new business opportunities. Often the tone of a search consultant's approach over the telephone is enough to guide you in what you choose to do about his invitations to lunch, for example. Generally, the harder the sell, the surer you can be that the firm's stature is less than tops. You may want to accept an invitation that sounds promising, and make it a Dutch treat, or decline an invitation that seems less likely to produce interesting information.

You can size up a search firm in much the same way that you size up job candidates. Just as you appraise actual candidates for employment in terms of their compatibility with the people they might be working with or for, appraise the search firm people you see. Some of them may be too young, too old, too didactic, too dynamic or too anything, to get along well with your key people whom they would be serving if given an assignment. Yet they may strike you as being highly compatible. Maybe they look good because of their previous company experience—someone who spent years recruiting executives for an international marketing organization of some company prominent in the field may hit things off very well with key people in your international marketing organization, for example. And you certainly want to note which ones strike you as being similar, themselves, to the kind of candidates you may be looking for. This is the sort of thing you want to keep notes on for your file.

By and large, you will find that search firm people are of a very high caliber. With relatively few exceptions they are people you would be glad to count as personal friends, on or off the job. So don't be a "one-way guy." Use your expense account, judiciously, to return favors and keep things on an even keel. The search consultants who particularly interest you should be worth taking out to lunch now and again, and should be worth introducing over lunch to one or another of your key executives, as potential service possibilities.

ADDING TO YOUR FILES

You should find out what the rules are in your company for assigning searches. Any time you assign a search you are incurring an expense that will grow steadily as time goes on, whether an acceptable candidate is referred or not, and these expenses can be sizable. Therefore, before committing yourself, find out who has to approve the search assignment in your company, and make sure that you have the necessary approval before you act. A certain amount of salesmanship may be involved. You may need recommendations from others in the company, or documented references for the search firm from other companies. Sometimes the final approval has to be given by someone such as your company president, even though the search firm will really be working to fill a job for someone at a lower level. In such cases, it is wise to first presell the lower level person, who will actually direct the search, on the merits of using an executive search firm, and then let that person help you sell the decision-makers.

In preparation for this selling job, it can be helpful to know which search firms are favored by your own key people. Find out which if any of the key people were recruited for your company by an executive search firm, and which search firms were involved. Obviously, any executive will have a warm spot in his or her heart for the search firm that brought him into a job that he likes. And it is a good selling point to say that a given firm was responsible for referring several of your top people to the company.

The reverse situation can be important, too, in the selection of a search firm—or nearly the reverse. Let's say that your assignment is to recruit a vice president, and the most important specification is that the candidate must be stronger than a principal assistant who will be reporting to that vice president. Who could understand this specification better than the search firm that referred the assistant concerned?

A good strategy is to ask your key people which search firms they think are most effective in special areas—whether the area concerned is financial, legal, international marketing, manufacturing or whatever. Their recommendations may lead to further conversation, as you bring in current information, such as, "You know, that firm has just been sold; they have a new president, new offices and are in a shakedown period now," or, "The man you mentioned came in to see me last week—he's just changed companies, but I understand he's still working in our field." Even if you have nothing to add, however, it is worth noting your own people's preferences, because it can add worthwhile information to your file on search firms.

PERSONNEL ASSOCIATIONS

Most personnel associations count among their members some search firm representatives. This should not be surprising, because a lot of the search firm people are former personnel executives. There are many other reasons for participating in personnel associations, but one of the advantageous by-products is that you are almost bound to meet some interesting search firm people this way. Some personnel associations, however, have rules that forbid taking in members who are currently in the search field. There are two reasons for this. First, since the membership and meeting expenses are usually met by the companies represented, there is a protective feeling about it—the supporting companies don't want to let people in who may recruit away the brighter personnel lights in the company. Second, you don't want to attend a professional association meeting and have to ward off people who are trying to sell their services to you. Just the same, if the search consultant has been a company personnel executive for a long time, and a member of the association for many years, most associations will "grandfather" him when he leaves his company affiliation and joins a search firm, because they figure (correctly in most cases) that he retains an active interest in the profession and has a lot to give to the association.

SEARCH FIRM OWNERSHIP

There may be occasions when you are conducting a search that has superconfidential aspects. For example, you may be looking for a new company president, and you don't want any word of it to leak out because the news could affect the price of your company's stock. In such a case, you may want to be particularly careful that the search firm with which you are dealing is wholly owned by the principals in the firm. It seems to be more and more popular today for investment banking houses and other firms closely related to Wall Street to buy into executive search firms. Although an arm's-length relationship, or an even more distant one, is probably typical in such a situation, you may just want to avoid any possibility that the confidence you share with the search firm may leak out to a third party. So pay particular attention to the ownership of any search firm that interests you, and avoid taking unnecessary risks in your search firm selection when it is important not to.

AGENCY SEARCH DESKS AND ONE-PERSON SEARCH FIRMS

One of the faults inherent in most directories or lists of search firms is that they tend to omit the employment agencies that offer competent executive search services as a sideline, and they tend to omit the one-person search firms. It is a serious omission, because there are many specialists who operate very successfully this way. You learn about them either by word of mouth, as you become acquainted with individuals who have dealt with them, or, occasionally, by finding them quoted in the business publications that serve your industry or functional groups. You have to be more than ordinarily careful, however, when you consider such people for search assignments. As there are no licensing regulations to prevent amateurs from setting up shop in the search field, and as the income from only a few successful searches, at 25 per cent of the first year's salary, will more than cover the needs of an average individual, there are a lot of people who try to take advantage of the income-producing possibilities in the search field. Entirely too many people become "consultants" when they are themselves between jobs, and the search business is one of the easiest consulting fields to enter.

One of the things you have to watch is the referral you get periodically from one of your own company executives. Any time you find yourself talking to a one-person search firm as a result of an in-company referral, be sure to follow up with your referral source. The question to ask is: "Did you send this person to me because you think very highly of him, or was it because you wanted to get rid of him without hurting his feelings?" Don't try to guess which answer applies.

WOMEN AND MINORITIES

If you are interested in finding a search firm that has special capabilities for recruiting women or minorities, there are two good sources of information. One is the person in the trade association that serves your industry who is specifically charged with promoting the employment of women and minorities.

Another source of information is your EEO Specialist or Compliance Officer, who comes around periodically to check up on your Affirmative Action Program performance. People in industry do not make enough use of the information these people can provide. If you just think about it, they spend all their time visiting the personnel and operating people in the other companies in your industry, and they know offhand the recruitment sources that have really done a job for your competitors.

More and more search firms today are establishing departments

More and more frequently these days, when a company is seeking to recruit a "new man," the best candidate may turn out to be a woman.

devoted specifically to the recruitment of female executives. Usually they are headed by women experienced in the recruitment and search business. Even those firms that do not have special departments for this purpose can usually turn up qualified candidates for you in the female and minority groups, if you ask them to do so.

DIRECTORIES OF EXECUTIVE SEARCH FIRMS

American Management Association, *The Executive Employment Guide.* This is a list of AMA member firms that provide executive search services, together with office addresses and a description of their services. Revised annually, it is a nine- or ten-page list in mimeograph or multilith, available for approximately $2. Write to AMA Management Information Services, 135 W. 50th St., New York, N. Y. 10020.

Association of Executive Recruiting Consultants, Inc., *Firms Doing Executive Recruiting.* Also known as the ACME (Association of Consulting Management Engineers) list of executive recruiting consultants. Periodically updated, it is a nine- or ten-page list of executive search firms that have been carefully checked by ACME and AERC, who vouch for their competence and ethics. Prepared primarily for job-seekers, it includes office addresses and is duplicated by office equipment. Free on request. Write to Association of Executive Recruiting Consultants, Inc., 30 Rockefeller Plaza, New York, N.Y. 10020

Jameson, R. J., *The Professional Job Changing System,* Performance Dynamics, Inc., 17 Grove Avenue, Verona, N. J. 07044. Published originally in 1970 and revised every two years, this is a hard-cover book containing much practical advice on how to get a better job. Includes a list of some 265 major executive recruiting firms and office addresses. Also some management consultants and CPA firms that provide search services. Available at Brentano's and most better bookstores for about $2.

McIntyre, R. J., *National Service Directory of Executive Employment Research,* 1972–73. Published by National Survey Information Co., Lake Bluff, Illinois 60044. Price available from the publisher. The unusual feature of this directory is a general performance rating on a numerical scale, assigned to each search firm listed. You may not agree with the rating given to a particular firm, but it can be useful when you are trying to locate a firm out of the country or in a domestic locale with which you are not familiar.

Performance Dynamics, Inc., *The Worldwide Directory of Job Changing Contacts.* Published by Performance Dynamics, Inc., 17 Grove Avenue, Verona, N. J. 07044. Available directly from the publishers for $10. This annual publication lists some 3,000 recruiters in all 50 states and 33 foreign countries, and is organized geographically by state and by country.

11
Concise Answers to Common Questions about Executive Search

Here are answers to the questions most often asked of executive search consultants by companies using or considering the use of the services of search firms.

How long does it take a search firm to fill an executive position?

Most searches take ten to twelve weeks to complete. Some positions have been filled in ten days or less; in other cases the assignment has taken fifteen months or more. It speeds things up when the client knows exactly the kind of executive he wants and is willing to spend enough of his own time to make an early decision. An extremely lengthy search usually has one of three causes: unusual or very difficult requirements from a technical point of view; the client's reluctance to pay the compensation necessary to attract qualified candidates; or a lack of agreement within the company on the kind of executive that is needed.

How much do the services of an executive search firm cost?

Most firms work for a fee of 25 to 35 per cent of the first year's compensation of the job being filled, plus out-of-pocket expenses. A few firms charge fixed fees or hourly time charges. Different fee levels may reflect different levels of experience brought to the assignment, as well as different overhead costs. For example, a search firm consisting of only highly experienced partners might charge higher fees than a firm using somewhat less experienced search consultants. Most firms bill one-third of the fee or estimated fee when the search assignment begins, one-third a month later, and one-third when the position has been filled.

What about contingency assignments in which the search firm gets paid in full after coming up with the right candidate?

You can find some search firms that will accept contingency assignments if they can't get your business any other way. The best firms, however, avoid such assignments partly because it is against the code of ethics of the Association of Executive Recruiting Consultants. Experience proves that contingency searches are seldom in anyone's best interest. They reward the search consultant for filling a position as quickly and cheaply as possible, rather than doing the extensive and thorough search that is almost always

necessary to uncover the best available candidates. It's a matter of luck rather than skill.

How much do out-of-pocket expenses run?

Figure 10 to 20 per cent of the fee per month on average during the course of the typical executive search. This sum includes travel expenses, costs incurred during the interviewing process, telephone charges, reference-checking costs, correspondence costs and other similar expenses. Expenses vary with the nature of the assignment, the type of executive required, where he lives relative to the client's home base, and the amount of search time involved. Travel, of course, is a big item, whether the search consultant goes to the candidate or the candidate comes to the search consultant.

How many qualified candidates does a search firm usually turn up for a particular position?

Depending on the nature of the job, a search firm may start by identifying dozens or hundreds of potential candidates. By the time it gets through weeding out and fine-screening prospects, however, there will probably be only three or four, possibly five, qualified candidates who are recommended to the client company.

How is the fee handled if we hire more than one candidate presented by the search firm?

In the case of a multiple search, where a company asks a search firm to fill two or more positions simultaneously, the assignments are usually considered separate, with separate invoices. In an individual search, it sometimes happens that, once the position is filled, the other candidates presented by the search firm will be so attractive that the client company will hire one or more of them for other positions. Usually when this happens, the search firm will charge a full fee for each position filled. A few search firms have established reduced fees for such situations, perhaps two-thirds of the normal fee when a second or third candidate is hired.

Suppose we retain a search firm but then find a qualified executive on our own, and hire him. What is our obligation to the search firm?

The search firm will, of course, terminate the search and usually will bill only for time spent up to that point, unless the initial letter of agreement specifies otherwise.

What happens if the executive selected from among the search firm's candidates does not work out?

Most search firms will replace an executive within one year at no charge—other than additional expenses—if early termination is deemed the fault of the search firm. For example, the search firm would take responsibility if the executive turned out to be incompetent or if there were a weakness in his character that should have been spotted. If the fault is attributable to the client company—for example, if the executive quits because the position turns out to be different from what the company told him it would be—then the search firm will not assume responsibility and will expect to be compensated for replacing the executive.

At what management levels do most companies use search firms to fill positions?

The rule of thumb is $25,000 a year on up. Because search fees are generally pegged to the size of the job to be filled, it is uneconomical for the client to use these specialized services below certain salary levels since the minimum fee would be disproportionate to the importance of the job being filled. Occasionally a company may find it worthwhile to offer a search firm a special fee for a particular low-level search. However, even search firms that concentrate on filling, say, $100,000 jobs will sometimes take on lower-level searches if their staffs are not fully loaded, or if the assignment comes from a long-term client.

What kinds of executives are companies usually seeking when they use search firms?

All kinds. Generalists and specialists. Some search firms take pride in handling challenging searches, for example, where candidates must have special industrial experience, special technical or functional know-how, second or third language proficiency, certain personality traits and so on.

Can search firms help us recruit competent women executives?

A prerequisite for recruiting women executives (and directors) is to provide within the company an atmosphere conducive to equal opportunity. This includes promoting qualified women already employed and avoiding stereotyped thinking as to what women can do. Once senior management has become dedicated to equal opportunity, the search firm can be of special assistance in finding women for key positions. While the law demands that women be considered for executive positions at varying levels, most organizations today lack women employees with both the education and experience required for key posts. Consequently, more organizations are looking outside for qualified individuals from the relatively small pool of talented female middle managers and top managers. To help such companies, some search firms have set up special departments to recruit women executives and directors.

How do we know the search firm we use won't raid our own executive staff?

It is a standard rule that search firms will not recruit executives away from their own clients. A client is usually considered to be any organization the search firm has served within the last two years. As a practical matter, clients are those organizations with which the search firm maintains an on-going relationship regardless of how long ago the last search was actually performed. If an executive from a client company approaches an executive search firm, the executive will be asked to get clearance from his superior before the search firm will consider him as a possible candidate. Sometimes a search consultant will ask an executive in a client company for advice in finding candidates for another client assignment. This is usually done without the executive knowing the name of the company for which the search is being conducted. If such an executive expressed personal interest in the position for himself, he would not be told the name of the client company, nor would he be considered a candidate. Some companies give their search assignments to a number of search firms in an attempt to keep their own executives from being recruited. This strategy may have limited effectiveness, but the fact is that if an outstanding executive wants to leave his company, or if he is qualified for a bigger job with more challenge and at higher rewards than that company can offer him, he will probably leave or be recruited regardless of how his company tries to shield him.

What guarantee do we have that a search firm, once retained, will produce satisfactory results?

The overwhelming majority of executive search firms offer no guarantees beyond their professional pledge to undertake a thorough search and to present qualified candidates. Just as there is no assurance that a lawyer will win his client's case or that a doctor will cure his patient's illness, there is no guarantee that the recruiter can complete every search assignment successfully. The growing reliance by business, government and other kinds of organizations on search firms attests that most searches are successful.

How can the search be kept confidential—or top-secret—so that members of our organization don't hear about it until we are ready to bring the new executive aboard?

Keeping a search totally confidential requires discipline and skill from both client and search firm. As few people within the client company as possible should know about the search—preferably no more than two or three. There are occasions where all written communications are sent to home addresses, and all meetings occur away from the client's offices. A top-secret search makes the job very difficult for the search firm. Although the identity of the client must be held back from all but the top two or three candidates, the search firm must impart enough information along the way to ascertain both the qualifications of the potential candidates and their true interest in the position. Once the client has been openly identified to the top two or three candidates, both the client and the search firm must be ready and able to move fast to make a final decision and a public announcement. It's the only way to avoid possible leaks, and it requires great synchronization, even a bit of luck.

Can a search firm help us define the kind of executive we really need?

Yes, this is an important part of the search firm's service. Based on tradition or a limited view of the executive job market, for example, a company may assume that a certain kind of executive is needed. A search consultant, with his broader, outsider's viewpoint, may be able to see that a different kind of executive will contribute more to the company's success. Usually, before any searching is begun, concise but thorough job specifications and man (or woman) specifications are drawn up and agreed to by all concerned. Perhaps understandably, some companies change specifications after they have interviewed candidates the search firm has recommended. In some cases, such changes may be unavoidable, but they are extremely costly and, for the search firm, extremely frustrating, since they may mean starting the search all over again. The sharper the search focus in the very beginning, the better for all concerned. Unfortunately, a surprising number of companies do not take the time to determine what kind of executive is needed. When this step is neglected, it often causes undue expense.

To what extent do search firms check candidates' references?

Skillful reference checking is one of the most valuable parts of the search firm's service. Experienced search consultants know the art of digging deep, rather than going through the perfunctory reference-checking procedure that is often considered adequate by nonprofessionals. Good reference checking takes time, patience, imagination, lots of hard work and skill. It also calls for the objectivity and guts to eliminate a candidate who looks great, and whom the client may favor, but whose reference checks show he won't fit, or won't succeed over the long pull. References are checked with the full knowledge of the candidate—depending upon methods used by individual search consultants—at various stages. Spot checks by telephone may be made early with the search consultant's contacts in the candidate's industry or trade association. As the search consultant becomes more seriously interested in the candidate, probably after more probing interviews, additional reference checks are made with previous employers and other business associates, both peers and subordinates. After client–candidate interviews, if questions remain unanswered in the mind of the client, further reference checks may be required, possibly with appropriate people in the company where the candidate is employed. How a good search consultant goes about the job of checking references is a subject in itself.

Do search firms use psychological testing or other such measurement methods?

Rarely if ever. Senior-level executives will seldom consider being tested. They do, of course, expect to be evaluated by present executives in the company. In exchange, most want the opportunity to size up the people in the company with whom they would be working. Experienced executive search consultants, whose work has brought them into contact with thousands of executives, develop their own evaluation methods. Formal psychological evaluation is almost always left to the client's discretion. If a client has doubts about the fitness of a candidate even after a search firm has proposed him, the search consultant may recommend psychological evaluation to substantiate the candidate's fitness. But it is unlikely that the search firm will use testing as part of its own selection process.

Shouldn't we use a search firm with specific experience in our industry?

Not necessarily. Some search firms do specialize in certain industries or management functions. Others find this self-defeating since they can't approach executives working for their own clients. The more clients they work for in the same industry, the fewer companies they have available as sources of candidates. Further, the skills, knowledge, techniques and strategies used by an executive search consultant are easily transferred from industry to industry. In this regard, the search consultant is like an attorney, accountant or management consultant. A good search consultant will uncover the best candidates in a particular field even though he may not have worked in that field before.

How does a search firm decide who in the firm will conduct the search?

In the case of a new client, the search firm will usually assign the search to the person whose experience most closely matches the requirements of the search. Personality will enter into it, too, of course, as will the work load of the search staff. The wise client, before the search is assigned, will be sure to meet the person in the search firm who will conduct the search, or direct it. Once a client–search firm relationship has been established, the same member of the search firm will usually be assigned to direct all search assignments from that client, since he is already informed about the nature of the client's business and management organization.

If a search firm has branch offices, do other offices participate in the search?

Generally, all of a search firm's offices are aware of all searches being conducted, except perhaps for the most sensitive ones. Usually, however, the search is conducted by the office that accepted the assignment, with the other offices participating by suggesting qualified prospects. For example, if the New York office of a search firm were seeking an oil executive, it would probably seek the help of its Houston office.

Do executive search firms work for companies that are direct competitors?

Yes. There are only a few industries where the number of important companies is so limited that it would be unethical for a search firm to serve more than one of them. Beyond these special industries, no problems arise as long as the search firm limits the number of companies served in a given industry to a few. In fairness, each client should be advised that the search firm's other clients are off-limits for recruiting. As for confidential information reaching a competitor through a search firm, no search firm would survive if it did not know how to handle sensitive and privileged information with the greatest discretion.

How long will a search firm go on searching if they have trouble turning up qualified candidates?

Most search firms will continue to work on a search until the client and the search firm together conclude that for one reason or another the position as specified is impossible to fill. However, when a search becomes difficult, it is seldom due to the search firm's inability to find candidates who meet the specifications. Rather, the problem is usually one of getting the client company and the candidate to come to terms. If there is an inherent shortcoming in the position itself, or if the hiring executive is not decisive, the chances of a successful search are greatly reduced. Nonetheless, most reputable search firms will work almost indefinitely to develop qualified and interested candidates.

Index